Lizzie McGuire

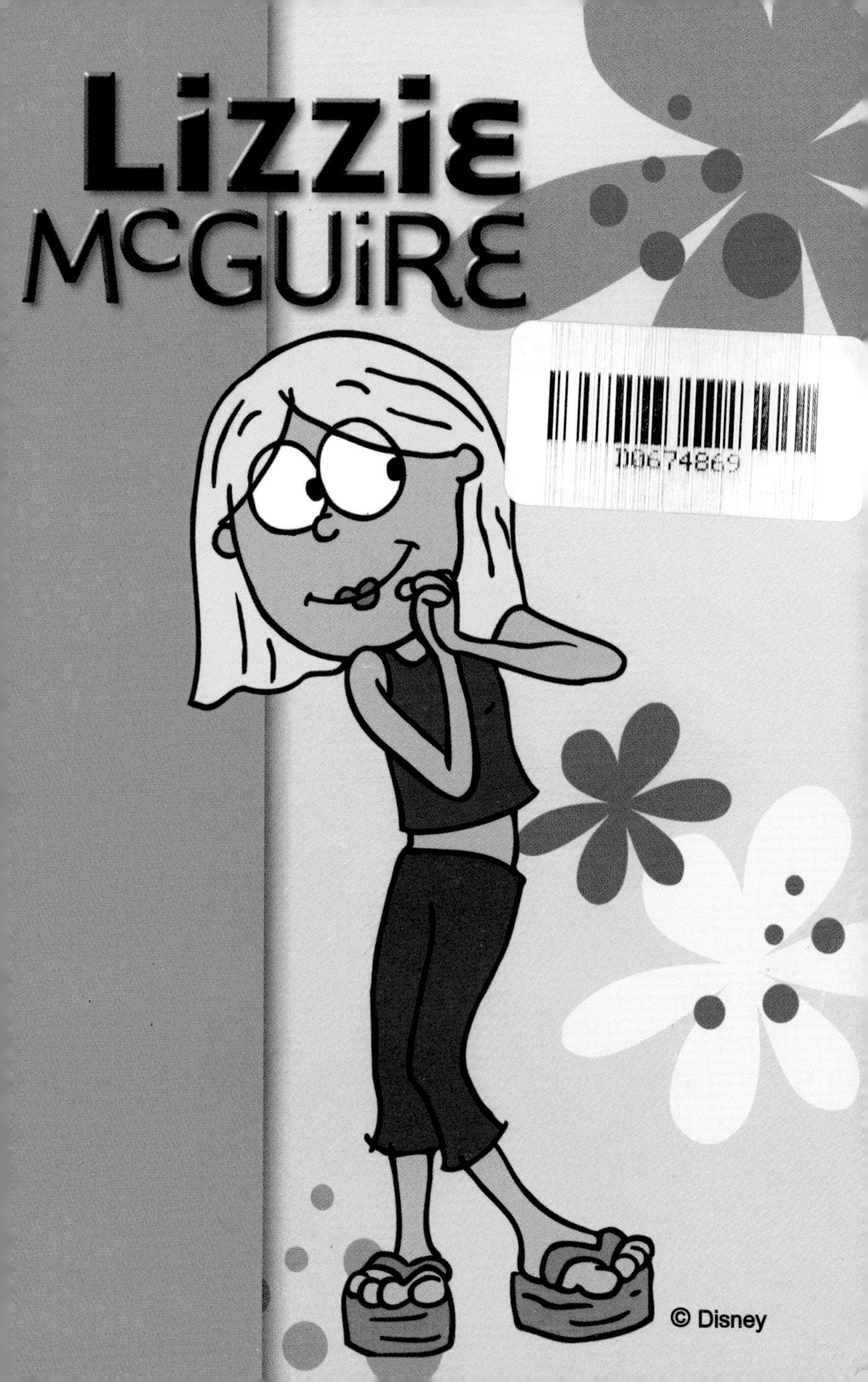

ALSO AVAILABLE FROM **TOKYOPOP**®

MANGA

.HACK//LEGEND OF THE TWILIGHT
ANGELIC LAYER*
BABY BIRTH*
BRAIN POWERED*
BRIGADOON*
CARDCAPTOR SAKURA
CARDCAPTOR SAKURA: MASTER OF THE CLOW*
CHRONICLES OF THE CURSED SWORD
CLAMP SCHOOL DETECTIVES*
CLOVER
CORRECTOR YUI
COWBOY BEBOP*
COWBOY BEBOP: SHOOTING STAR*
CYBORG 009*
DEMON DIARY
DIGIMON*
DRAGON HUNTER
DRAGON KNIGHTS*
DUKLYON: CLAMP SCHOOL DEFENDERS*
FLCL*
FORBIDDEN DANCE*
GATE KEEPERS*
G GUNDAM*
GRAVITATION*
GUNDAM WING
GUNDAM WING: BATTLEFIELD OF PACIFISTS
GUNDAM WING: ENDLESS WALTZ*
GUNDAM WING: THE LAST OUTPOST*
HARLEM BEAT
I.N.V.U.
INITIAL D*
JING: KING OF BANDITS*
JULINE
KARE KANO*
KINDAICHI CASE FILES, THE*
KING OF HELL
KODOCHA: SANA'S STAGE*

MAGIC KNIGHT RAYEARTH*
MAGIC KNIGHT RAYEARTH II* (COMING SOON)
MAN OF MANY FACES*
MARMALADE BOY*
MARS*
MIRACLE GIRLS
MONSTERS, INC.
PEACH GIRL
PEACH GIRL: CHANGE OF HEART*
PET SHOP OF HORRORS*
PLANET LADDER*
PLANETES* (October 2003)
RAGNAROK
RAVE MASTER*
REALITY CHECK!
REBIRTH
REBOUND*
RISING STARS OF MANGA
SAILOR MOON
SAINT TAIL
SAMURAI GIRL: REAL BOUT HIGH SCHOOL*
SHAOLIN SISTERS*
SHIRAHIME-SYO: SNOW GODDESS TALES* (Dec. 2003)
THE SKULL MAN*
THE VISION OF ESCAFLOWNE
TOKYO MEW MEW*
VAMPIRE GAME*
WISH*
WORLD OF HARTZ (October 2003)
ZODIAC P.I.*

*INDICATES 100% AUTHENTIC MANGA (RIGHT-TO-LEFT FORMAT)

CINE-MANGA™

CARDCAPTORS
JACKIE CHAN ADVENTURES (COMING SOON)
JIMMY NEUTRON
KIM POSSIBLE
LIZZIE MCGUIRE
POWER RANGERS: NINJA STORM
SPONGEBOB SQUAREPANTS
SPY KIDS 2

NOVELS

KARMA CLUB (April 2004)
SAILOR MOON

TOKYOPOP KIDS

STRAY SHEEP

ART BOOKS

CARDCAPTOR SAKURA*
MAGIC KNIGHT RAYEARTH*

ANIME GUIDES

COWBOY BEBOP ANIME GUIDES
GUNDAM TECHNICAL MANUALS
SAILOR MOON SCOUT GUIDES   062703
For more information visit www.TOKYOPOP.com

Lizzie McGuire

Volume 3

Series created by Terri Minsky

"When Moms Attack"
written by Nina G. Bargiel & Jeremy J. Bargiel

"Misadventures in Babysitting"
written by David Blum & Stacy Kramer

TOKYOPOP®

LOS ANGELES • TOKYO • LONDON

Contributing Editors - Paul Morrissey & Kimberlee Smith
Graphic Design & Lettering - Yolanda Petriz
Production Specialists - Anna Kernbaum
& Tomás Montalvo-Lagos
Cover Layout - Patrick Hook

Editor - Elizabeth Hurchalla
Managing Editor - Jill Freshney
Production Coordinator - Antonio DePietro
Production Manager - Jennifer Miller
Art Director - Matt Alford
Editorial Director - Jeremy Ross
VP of Production - Ron Klamert
President & C.O.O. - John Parker
Publisher & C.E.O. - Stuart Levy

Email: editor@TOKYOPOP.com
Come visit us online at www.TOKYOPOP.com

A **TOKYOPOP**® Cine-Manga™
5900 Wilshire Blvd., Suite 2000, Los Angeles, CA 90036

ISBN: 1-59182-245-9

First TOKYOPOP printing: November 2003

10 9 8 7 6 5 4 3 2 1

Printed in Canada

Lizzie
McGuire

Volume 3

CONTENTS

Lizzie McGuire

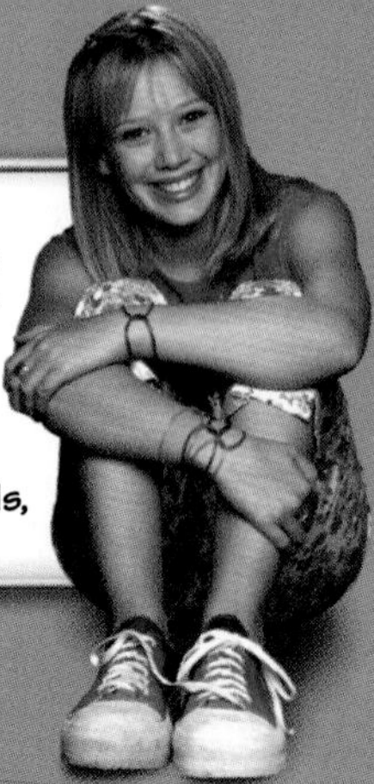

LIZZIE MCGUIRE
A typical 14-year-old girl who has her fair share of bad hair days and embarrassing moments. Luckily, Lizzie knows how to admit when she's wrong, back up her friends, and stand up for herself.

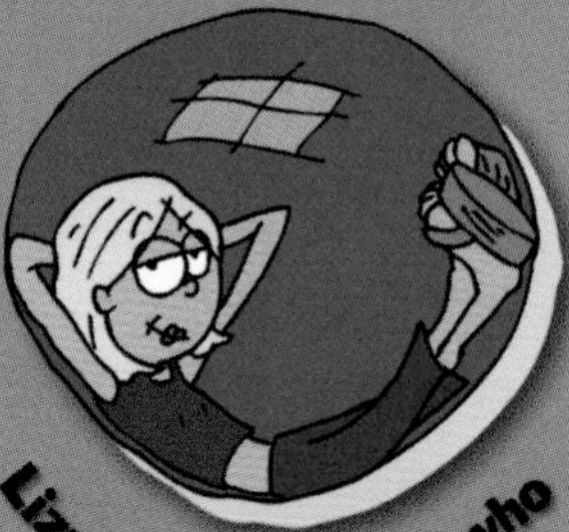

Lizzie's alter-ego, who says and does all the things Lizzie's afraid to.

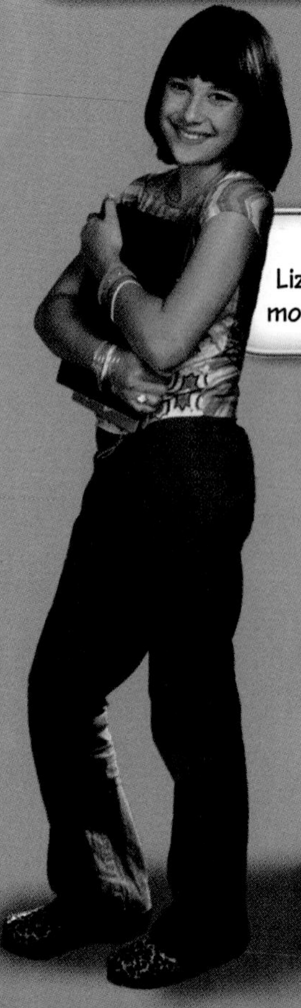

MIRANDA
Lizzie's best friend and most trusted confidante.

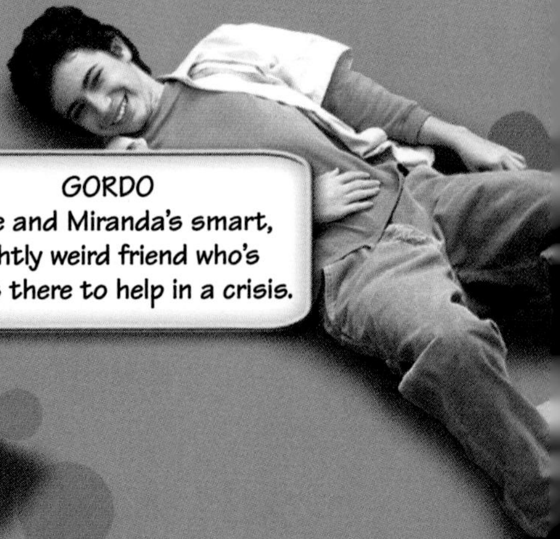

GORDO
Lizzie and Miranda's smart, slightly weird friend who's always there to help in a crisis.

KATE
Lizzie and Miranda's ex-friend who thinks she's too good for them now that she wears a bra.

MR. PETTUS
Lizzie, Gordo, and Miranda's science teacher.

MATT
Lizzie's little brother, who spends most of his time driving her crazy.

LIZZIE'S MOM, JO
She only wants the best for Lizzie, but sometimes she tries a little too hard.

LIZZIE'S DAD, SAM
He loves Lizzie, though he doesn't always know how to relate to her.

Lizzie McGuire

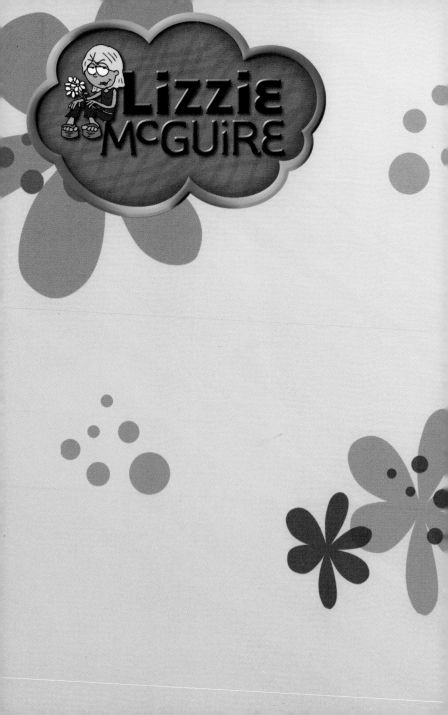

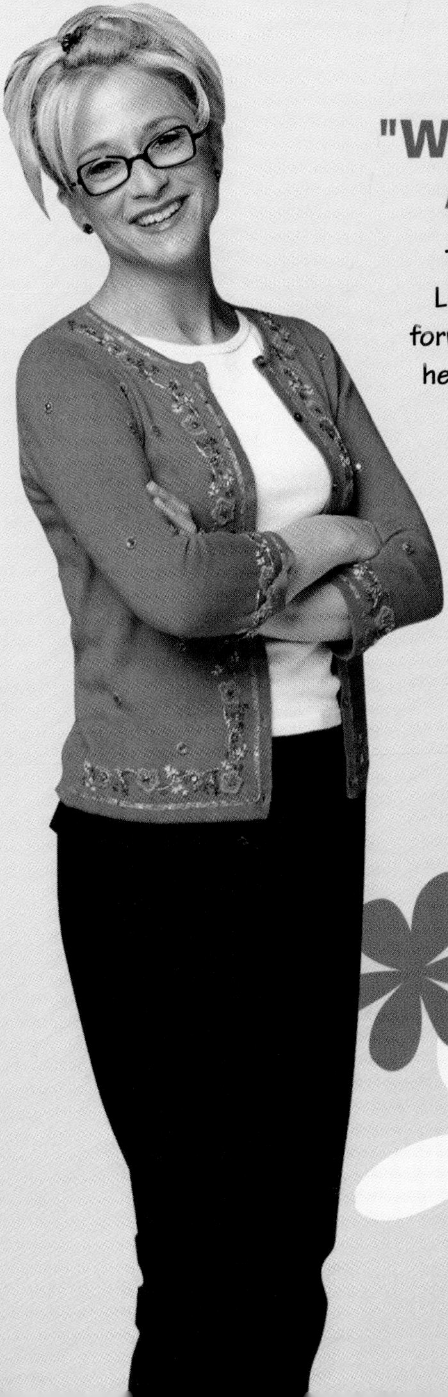

Episode 5

"When Moms Attack"

The class field trip Lizzie's been looking forward to turns into her worst nightmare when her mother comes along as a replacement chaperone!

LIZZIE'S ROOM...

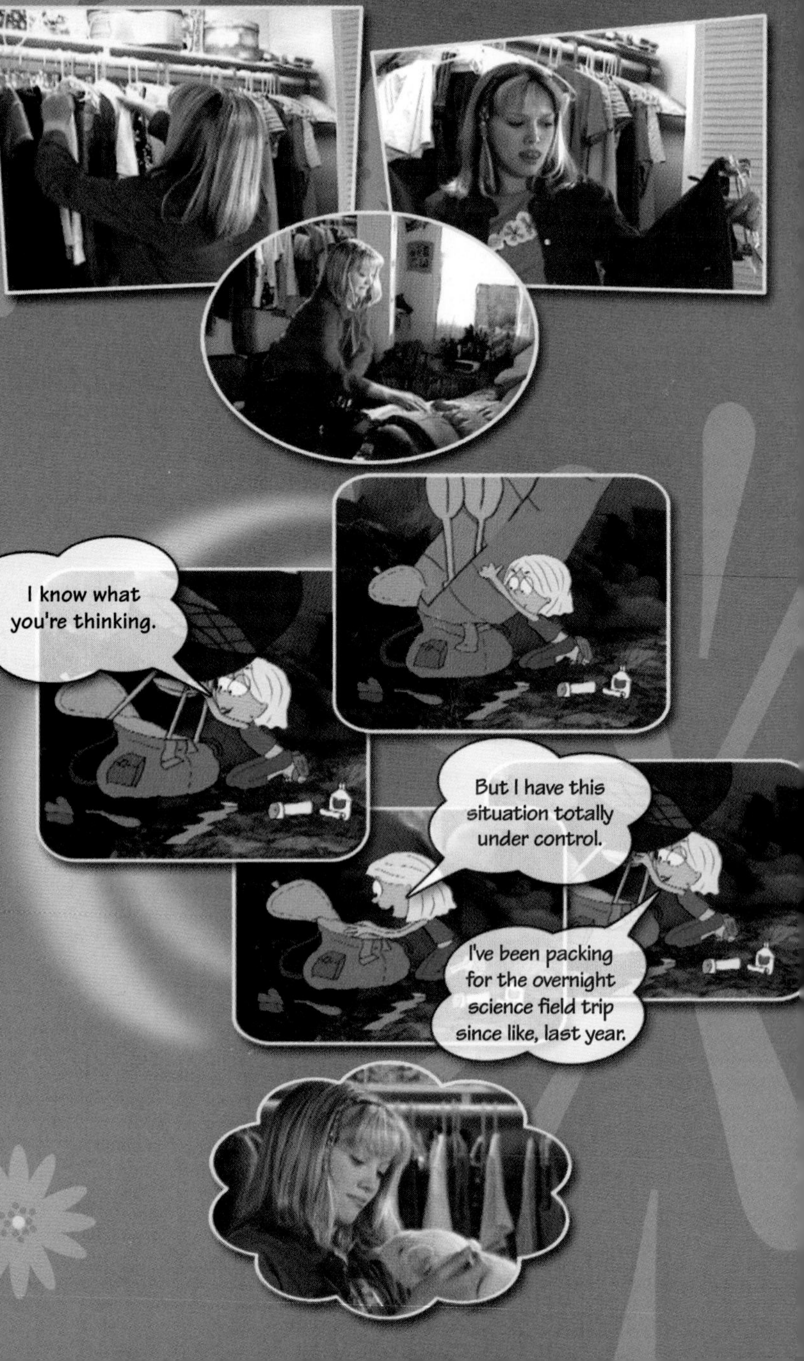
I know what you're thinking.
But I have this situation totally under control.
I've been packing for the overnight science field trip since like, last year.

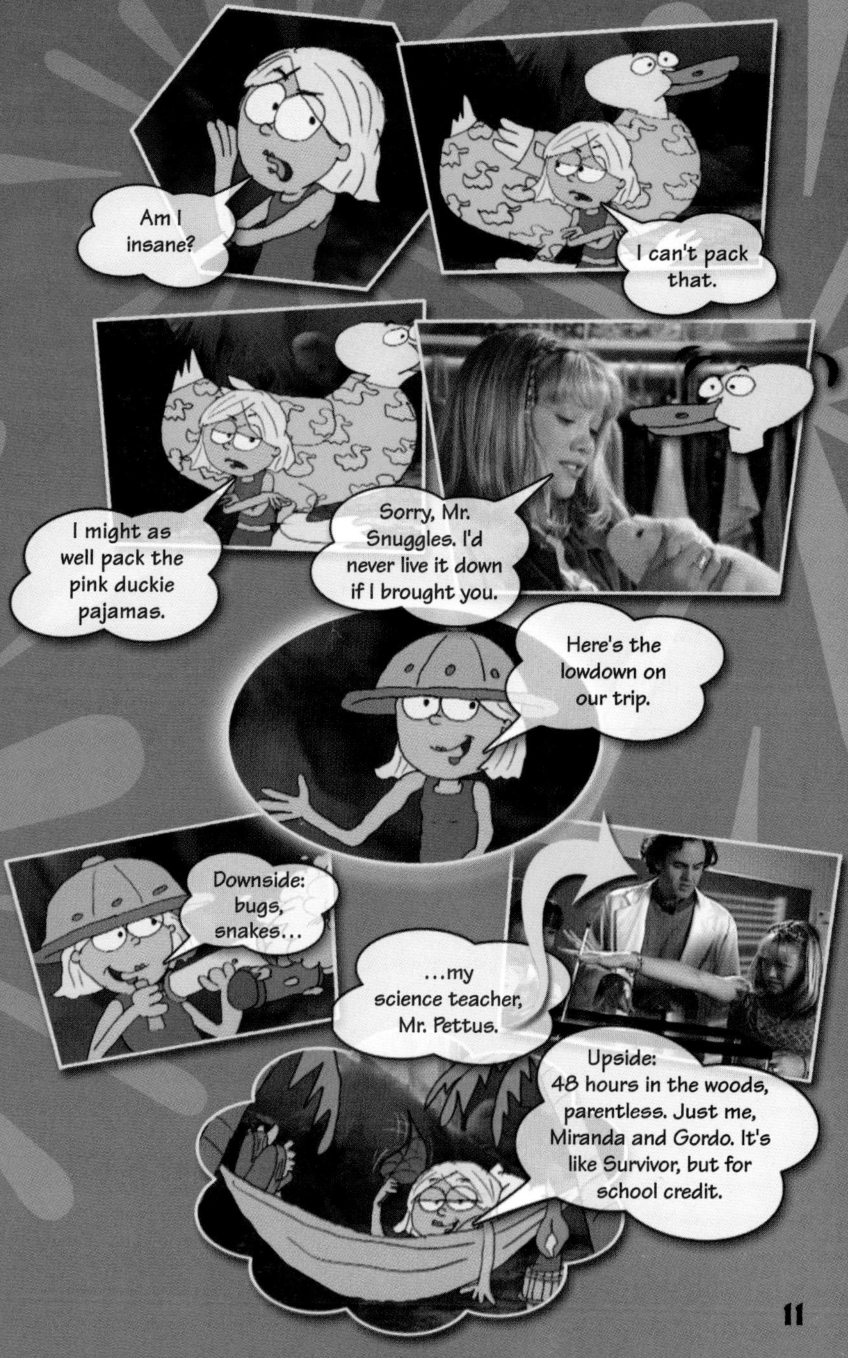
Am I insane?
I can't pack that.
I might as well pack the pink duckie pajamas.
Sorry, Mr. Snuggles. I'd never live it down if I brought you.
Here's the lowdown on our trip.
Downside: bugs, snakes...
...my science teacher, Mr. Pettus.
Upside: 48 hours in the woods, parentless. Just me, Miranda and Gordo. It's like Survivor, but for school credit.

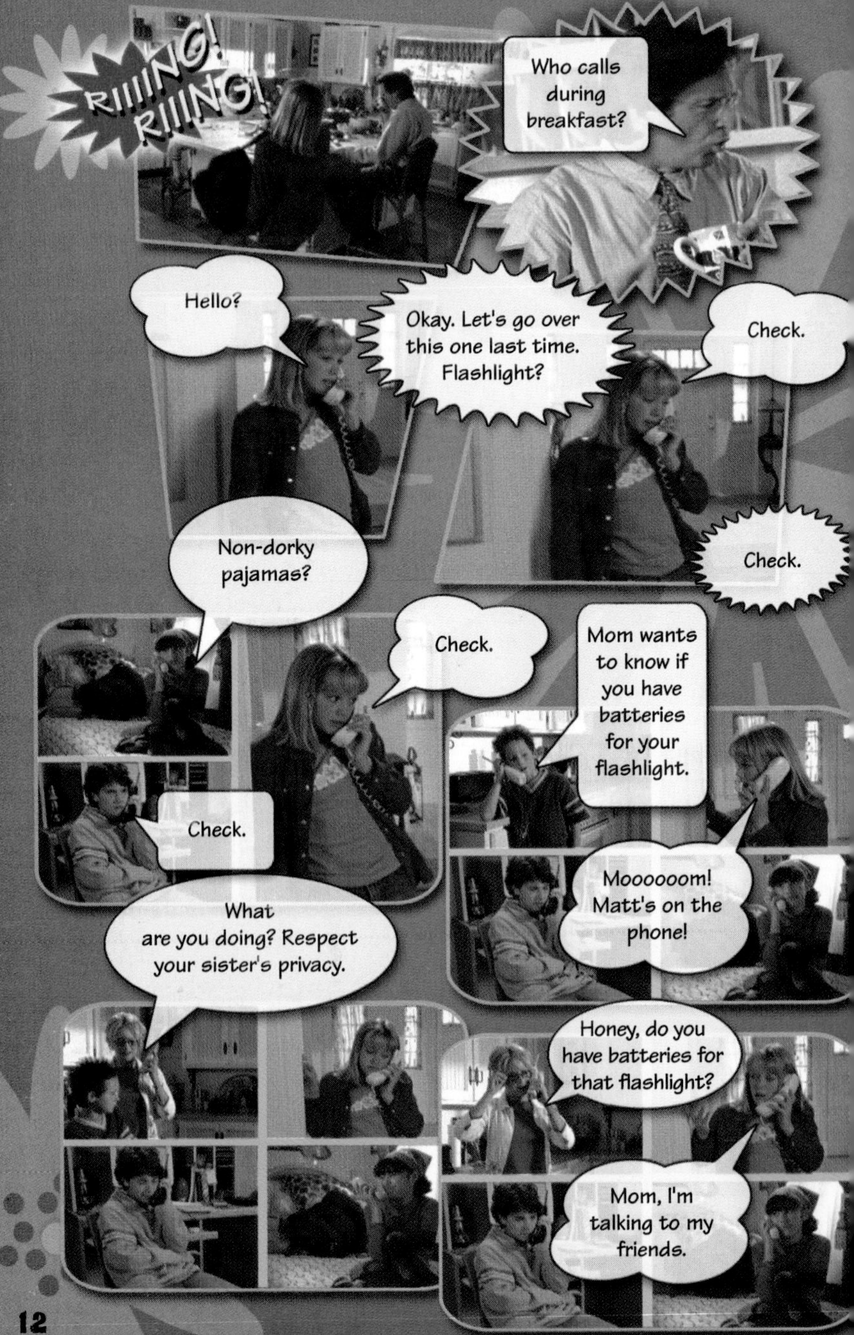
RIIIING! RIIING!
Who calls during breakfast?
Hello?
Okay. Let's go over this one last time. Flashlight?
Check.
Non-dorky pajamas?
Check.
Check.
Check.
Mom wants to know if you have batteries for your flashlight.
Moooooom! Matt's on the phone!
What are you doing? Respect your sister's privacy.
Honey, do you have batteries for that flashlight?
Mom, I'm talking to my friends.

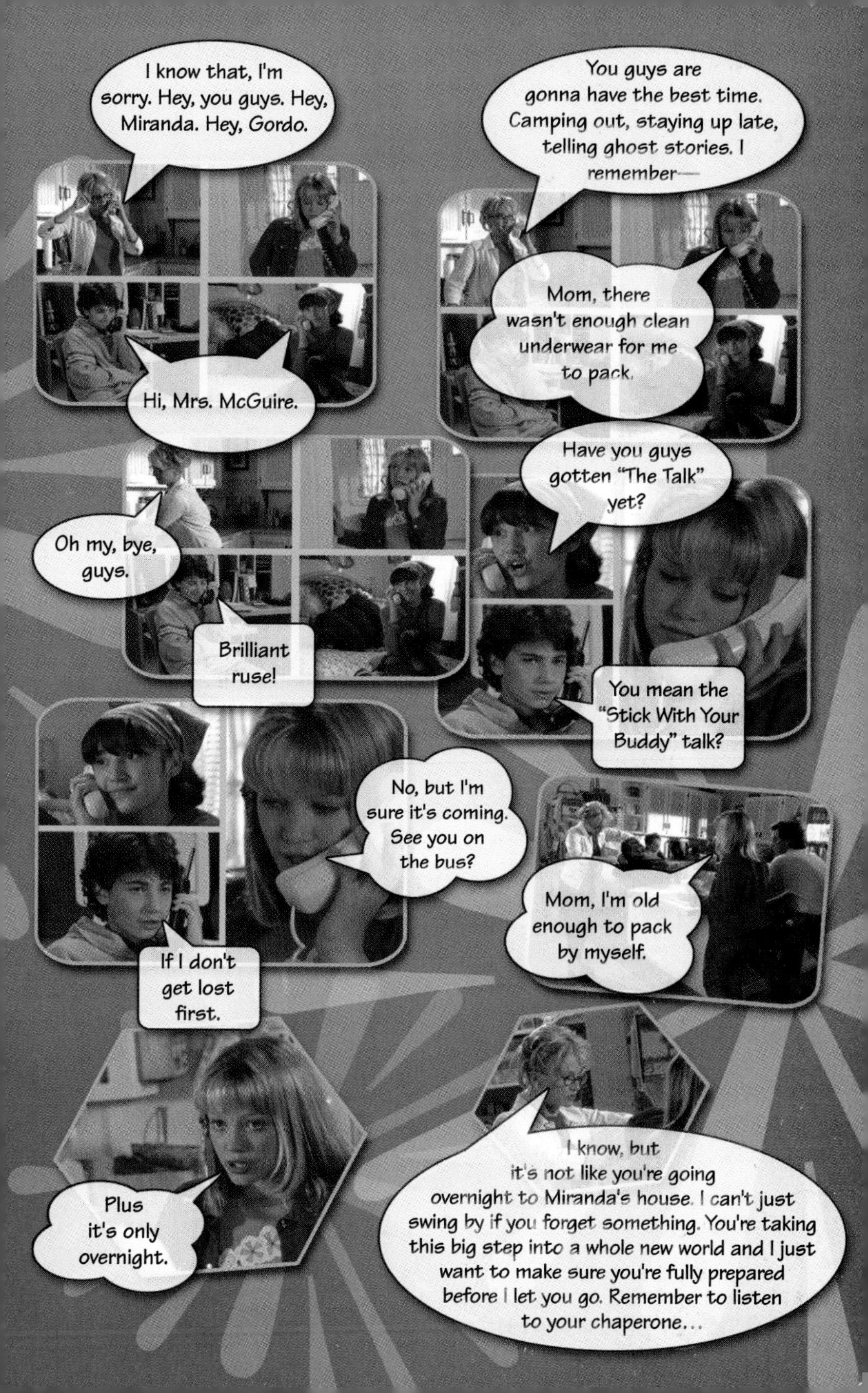
I know that, I'm sorry. Hey, you guys. Hey, Miranda. Hey, Gordo.
Hi, Mrs. McGuire.
You guys are gonna have the best time. Camping out, staying up late, telling ghost stories. I remember—
Mom, there wasn't enough clean underwear for me to pack.
Oh my, bye, guys.
Brilliant ruse!
Have you guys gotten "The Talk" yet?
You mean the "Stick With Your Buddy" talk?
No, but I'm sure it's coming. See you on the bus?
If I don't get lost first.
Mom, I'm old enough to pack by myself.
Plus it's only overnight.
I know, but it's not like you're going overnight to Miranda's house. I can't just swing by if you forget something. You're taking this big step into a whole new world and I just want to make sure you're fully prepared before I let you go. Remember to listen to your chaperone...

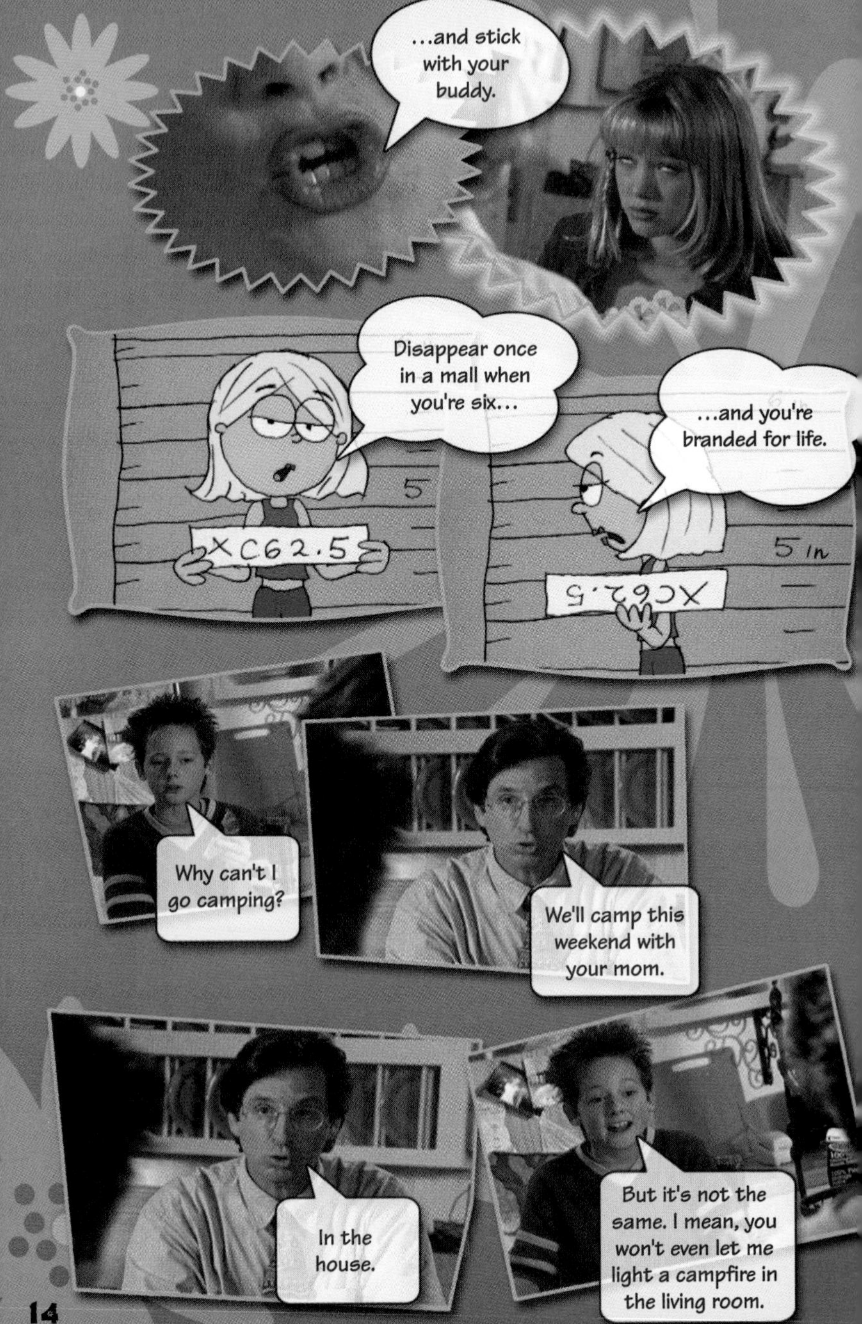
...and stick with your buddy.
Disappear once in a mall when you're six...
...and you're branded for life.
XC62.5
5
5 in
Why can't I go camping?
We'll camp this weekend with your mom.
In the house.
But it's not the same. I mean, you won't even let me light a campfire in the living room.

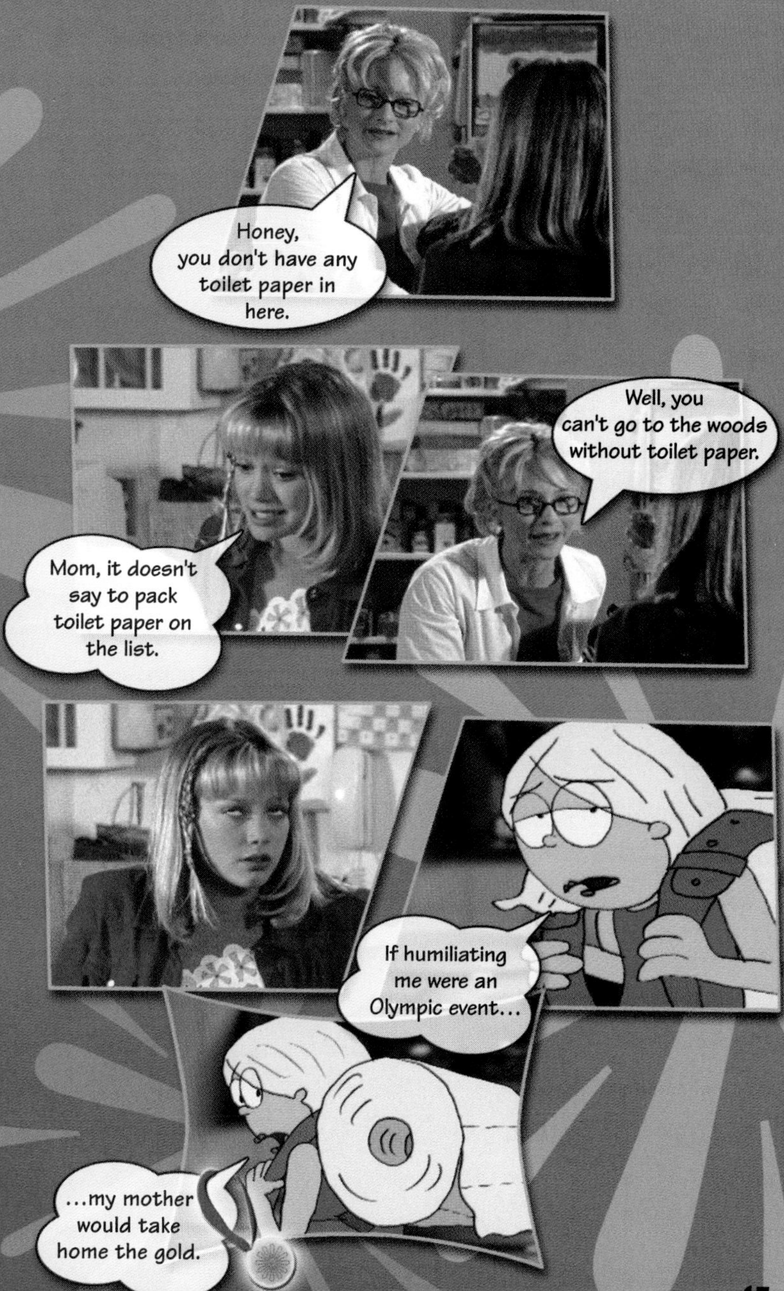
Honey, you don't have any toilet paper in here.
Mom, it doesn't say to pack toilet paper on the list.
Well, you can't go to the woods without toilet paper.
If humiliating me were an Olympic event...
...my mother would take home the gold.

LATER AT SCHOOL...

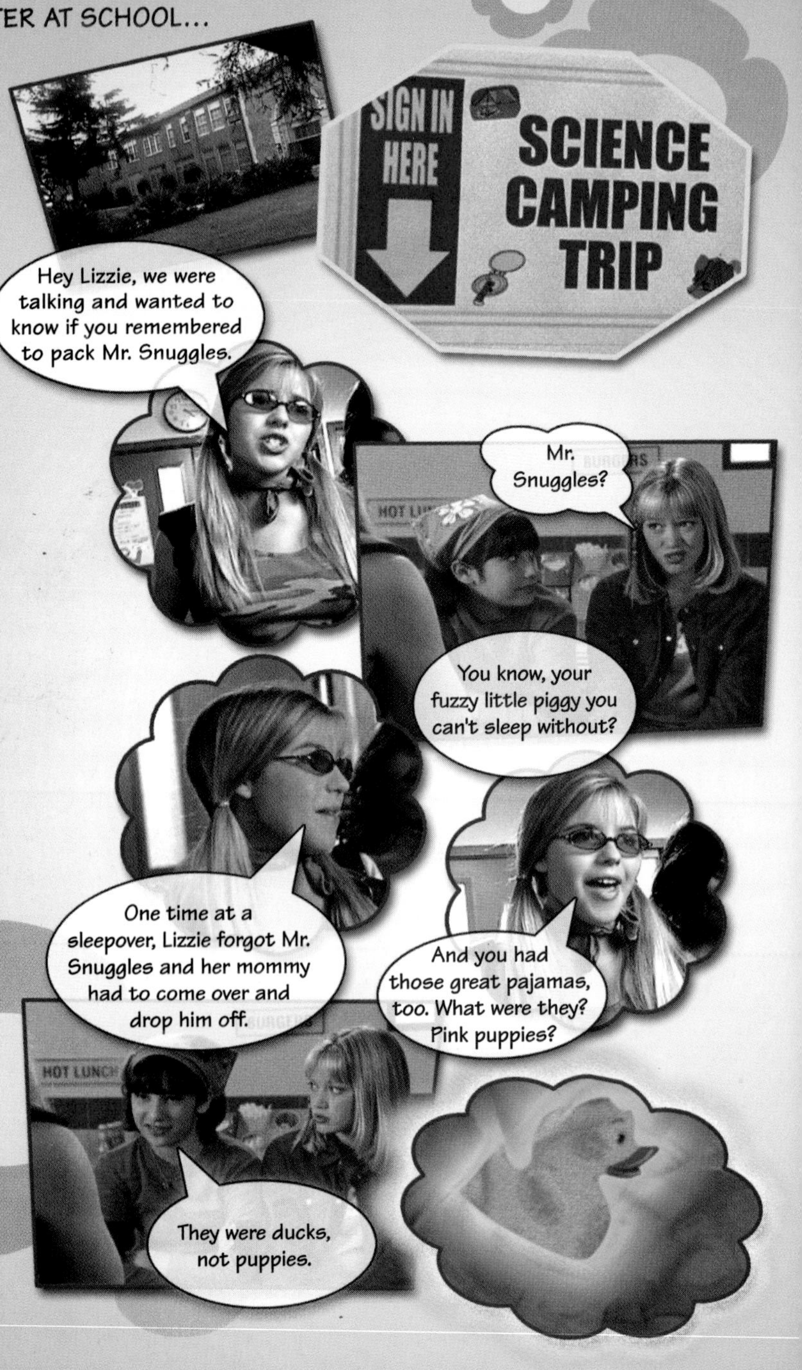
SIGN IN HERE
SCIENCE CAMPING TRIP
Hey Lizzie, we were talking and wanted to know if you remembered to pack Mr. Snuggles.
Mr. Snuggles?
You know, your fuzzy little piggy you can't sleep without?
One time at a sleepover, Lizzie forgot Mr. Snuggles and her mommy had to come over and drop him off.
And you had those great pajamas, too. What were they? Pink puppies?
They were ducks, not puppies.

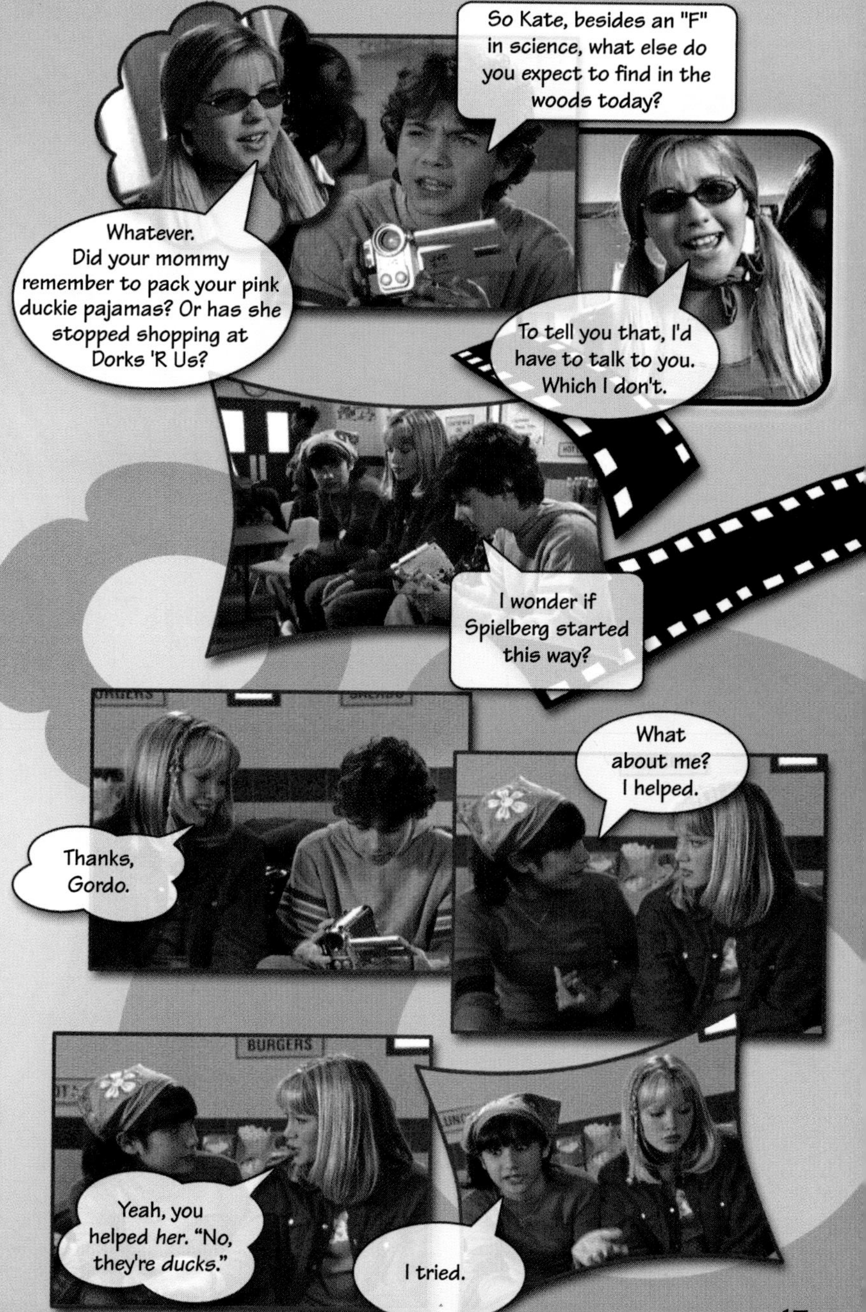

So Kate, besides an "F" in science, what else do you expect to find in the woods today?
Whatever. Did your mommy remember to pack your pink duckie pajamas? Or has she stopped shopping at Dorks 'R Us?
To tell you that, I'd have to talk to you. Which I don't.
I wonder if Spielberg started this way?
Thanks, Gordo.
What about me? I helped.
BURGERS
Yeah, you helped *her*. "No, they're *ducks*."
I tried.

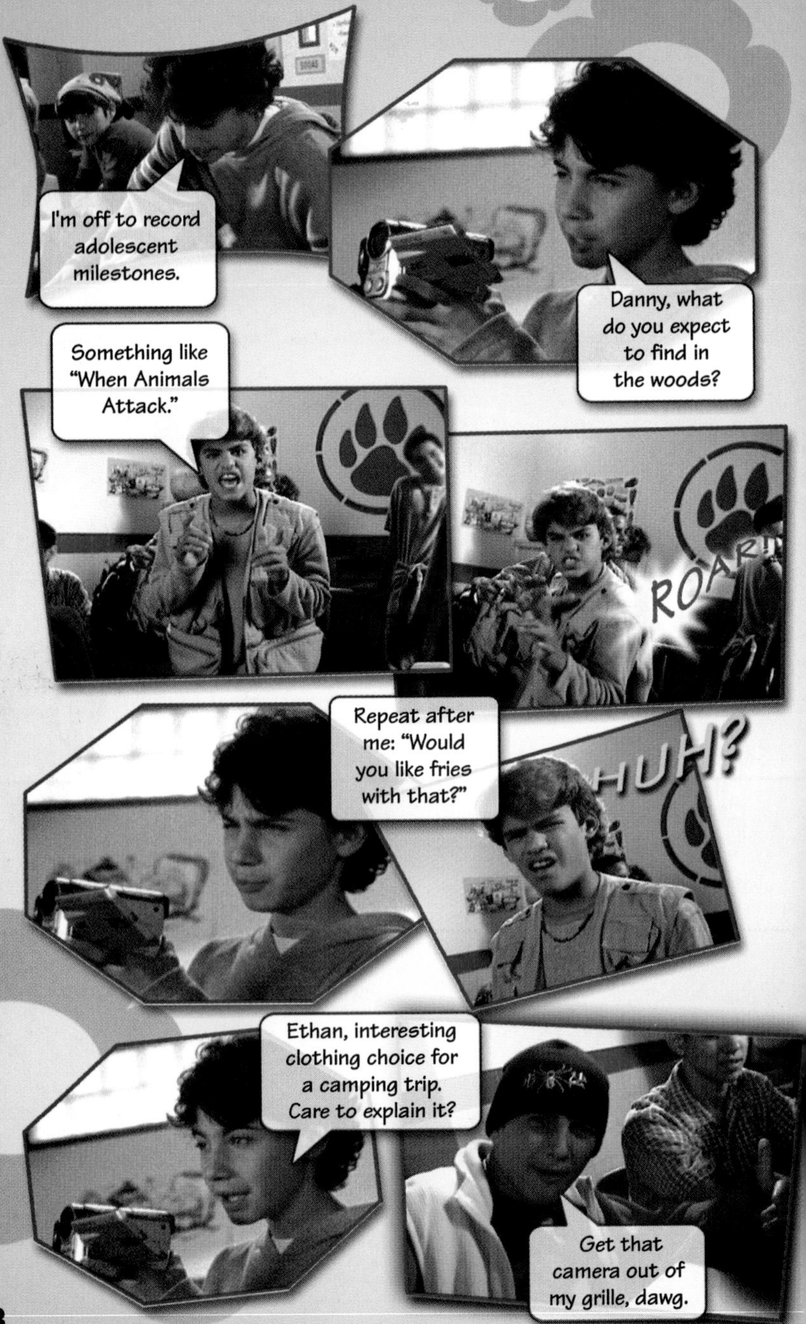

I'm off to record adolescent milestones.
Danny, what do you expect to find in the woods?
Something like "When Animals Attack."
ROAR!
Repeat after me: "Would you like fries with that?"
HUH?
Ethan, interesting clothing choice for a camping trip. Care to explain it?
Get that camera out of my grille, dawg.

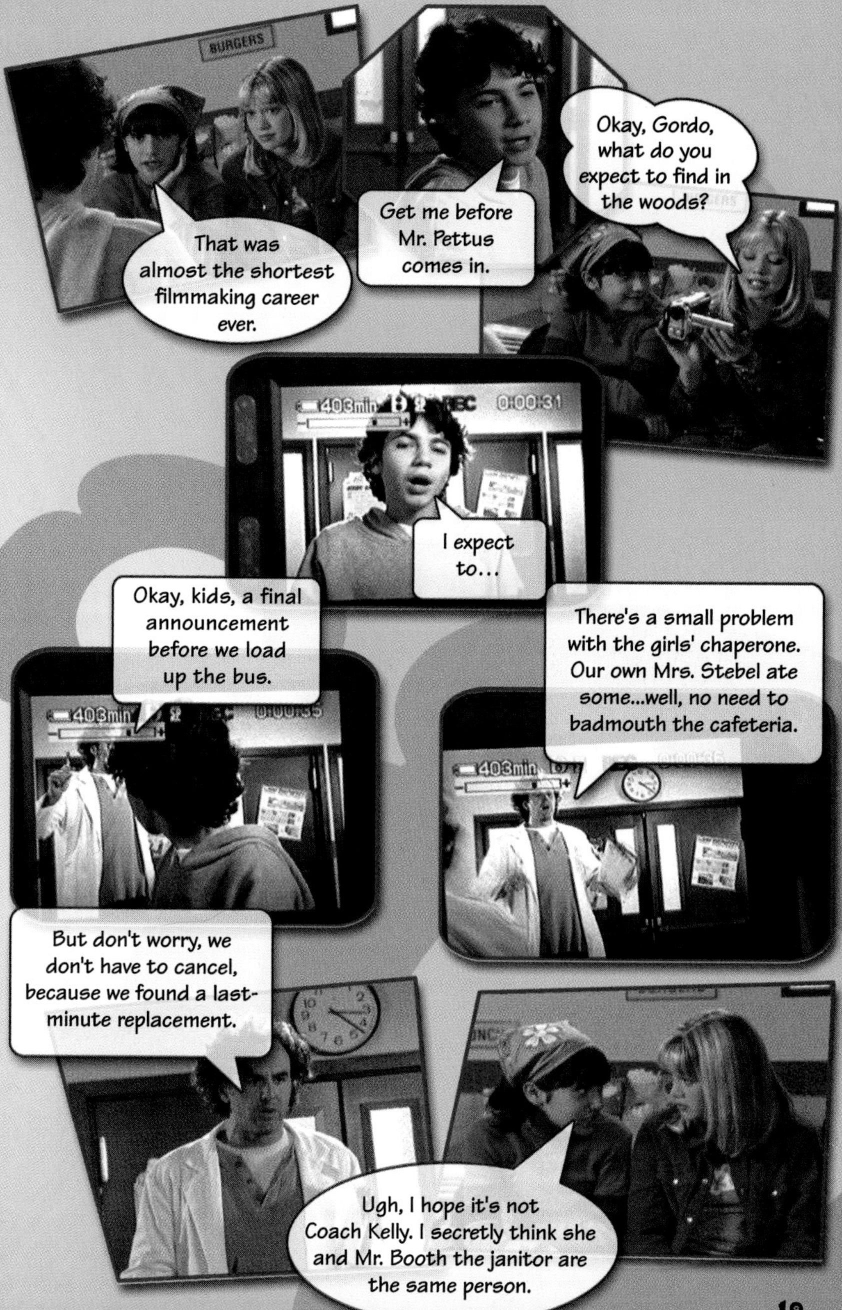
That was almost the shortest filmmaking career ever.
Get me before Mr. Pettus comes in.
Okay, Gordo, what do you expect to find in the woods?
I expect to…
Okay, kids, a final announcement before we load up the bus.
There's a small problem with the girls' chaperone. Our own Mrs. Stebel ate some...well, no need to badmouth the cafeteria.
But don't worry, we don't have to cancel, because we found a last-minute replacement.
Ugh, I hope it's not Coach Kelly. I secretly think she and Mr. Booth the janitor are the same person.

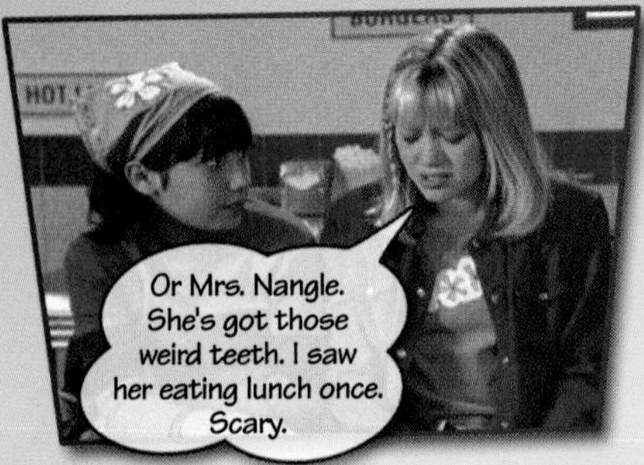
Or Mrs. Nangle. She's got those weird teeth. I saw her eating lunch once. Scary.

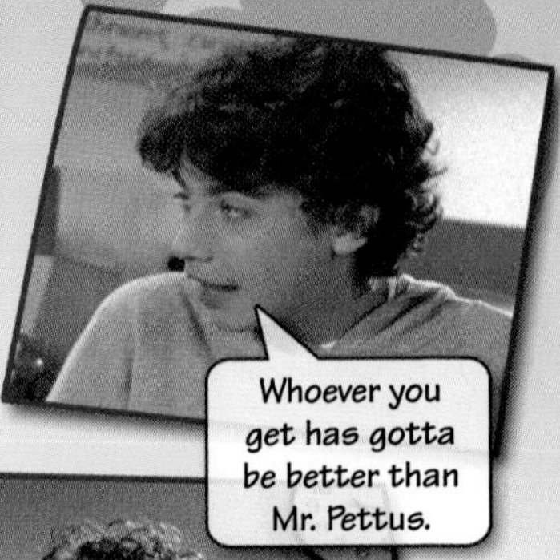
Whoever you get has gotta be better than Mr. Pettus.

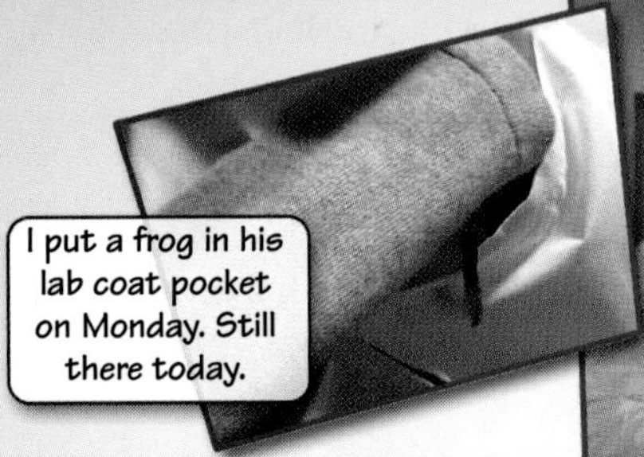
I put a frog in his lab coat pocket on Monday. Still there today.

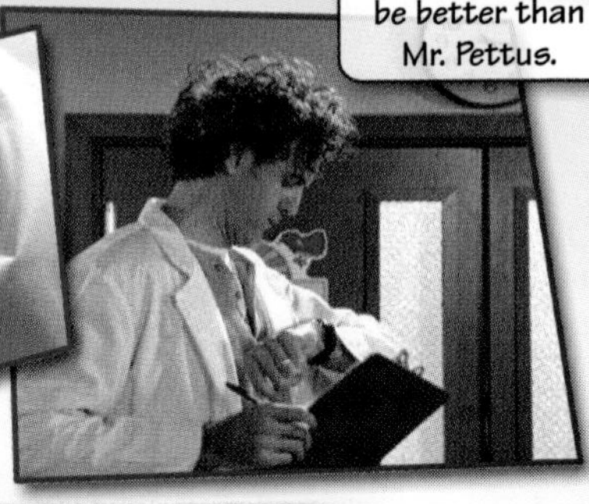

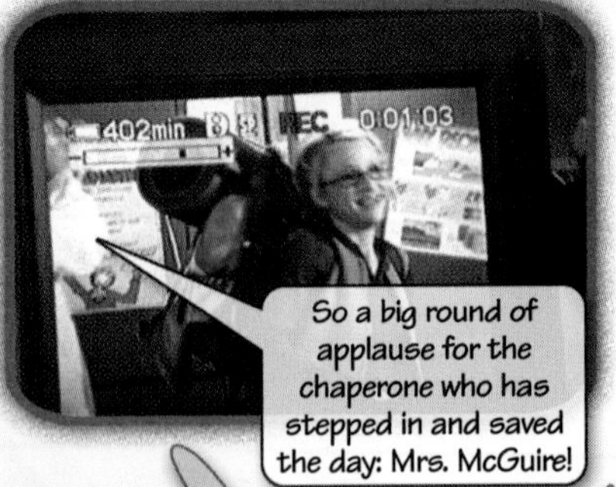
402min
REC
0:01:03
So a big round of applause for the chaperone who has stepped in and saved the day: Mrs. McGuire!

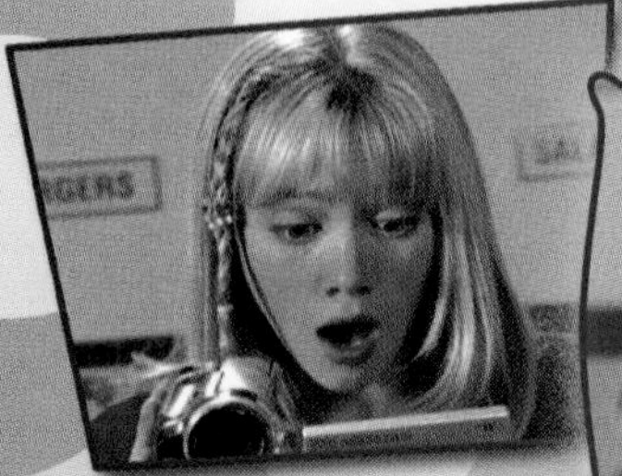

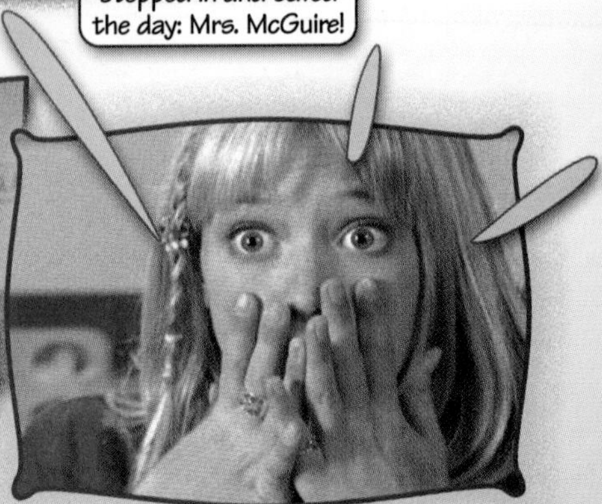

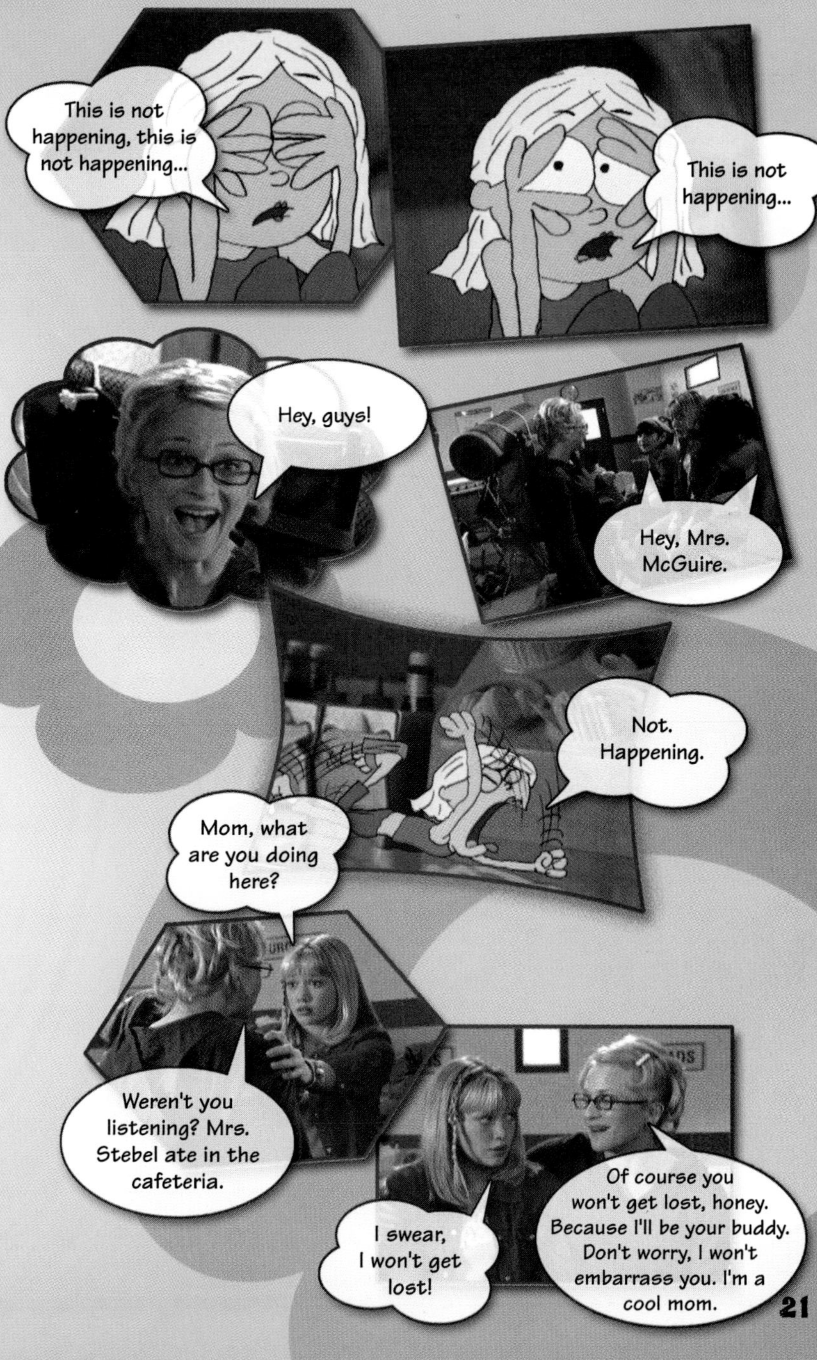
This is not happening, this is not happening...
This is not happening...
Hey, guys!
Hey, Mrs. McGuire.
Not. Happening.
Mom, what are you doing here?
Weren't you listening? Mrs. Stebel ate in the cafeteria.
I swear, I won't get lost!
Of course you won't get lost, honey. Because I'll be your buddy. Don't worry, I won't embarrass you. I'm a cool mom.

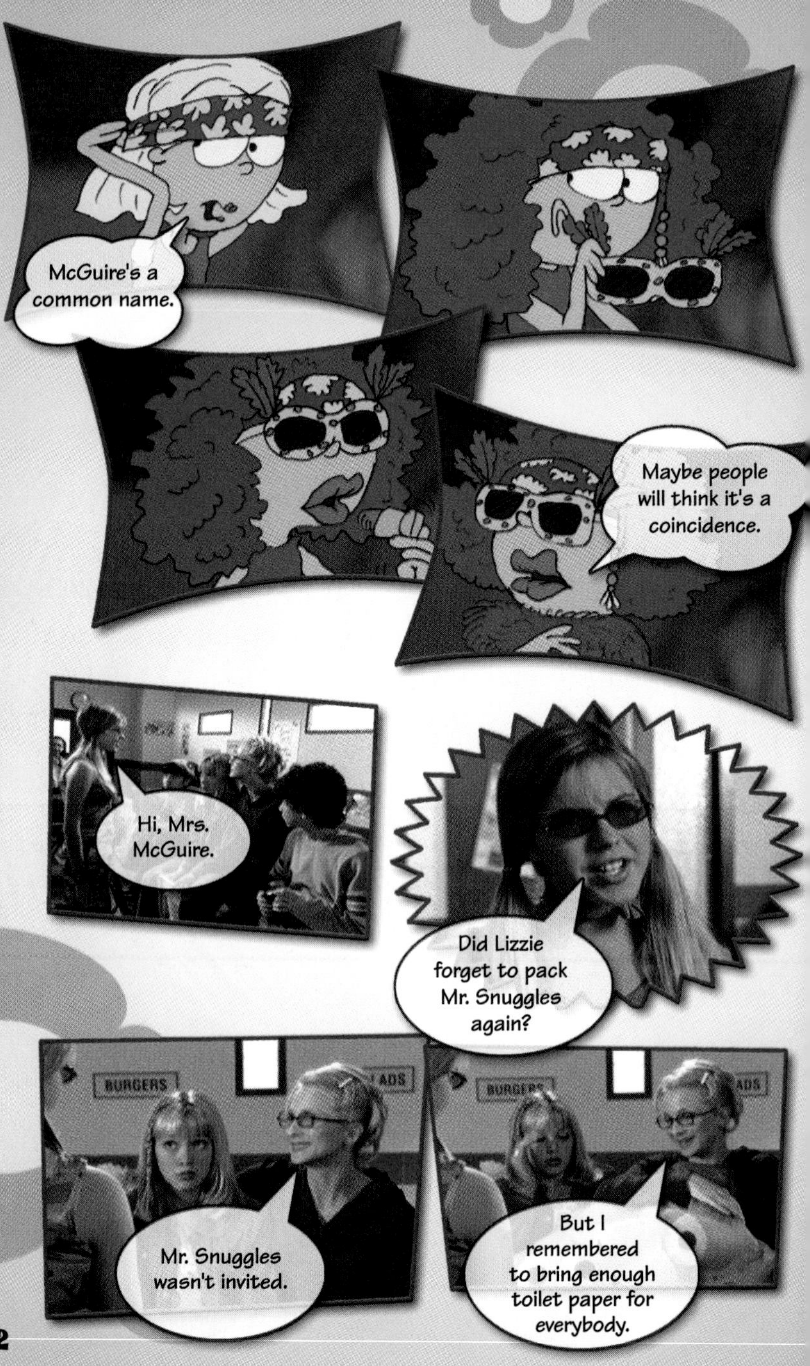
McGuire's a common name.
Maybe people will think it's a coincidence.
Hi, Mrs. McGuire.
Did Lizzie forget to pack Mr. Snuggles again?
BURGERS
Mr. Snuggles wasn't invited.
But I remembered to bring enough toilet paper for everybody.

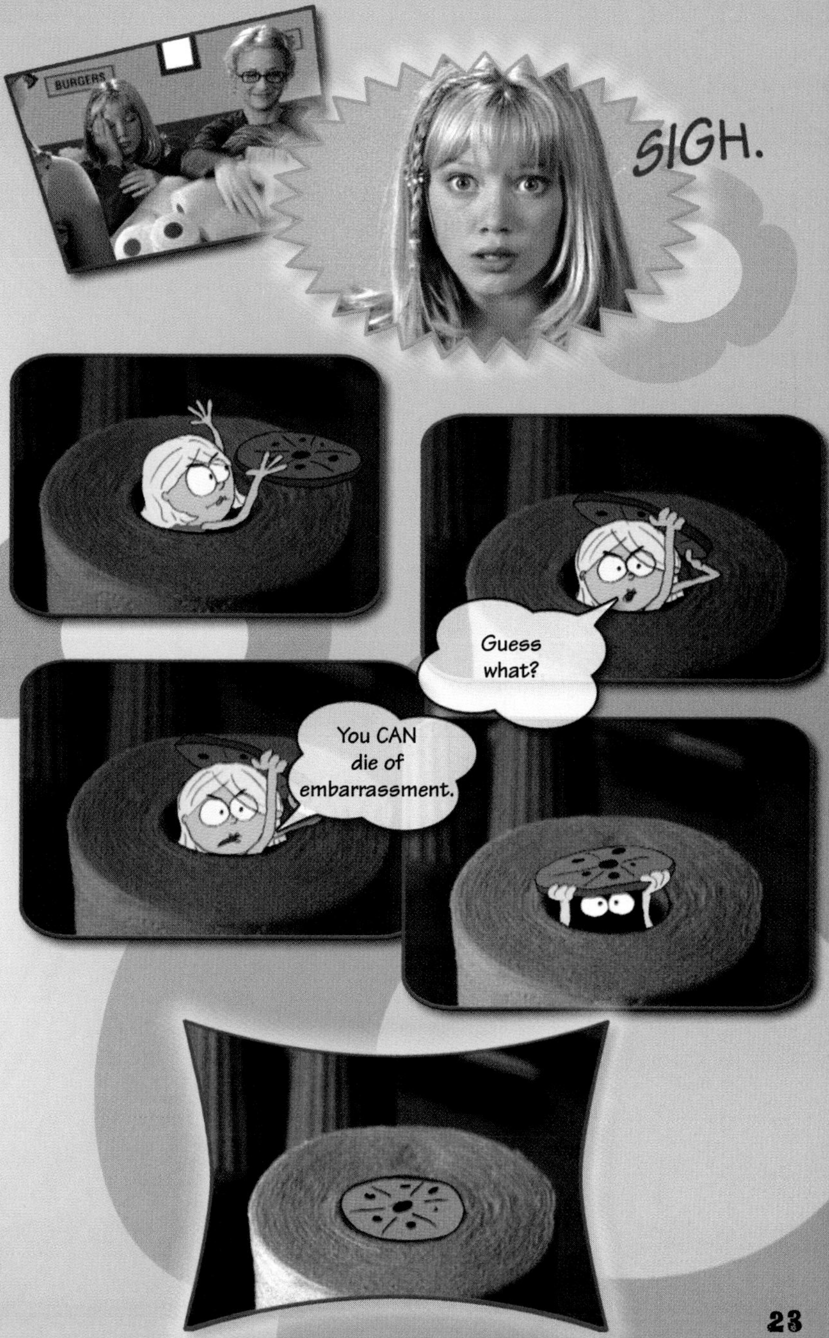
BURGERS
SIGH.
Guess what?
You CAN die of embarrassment.

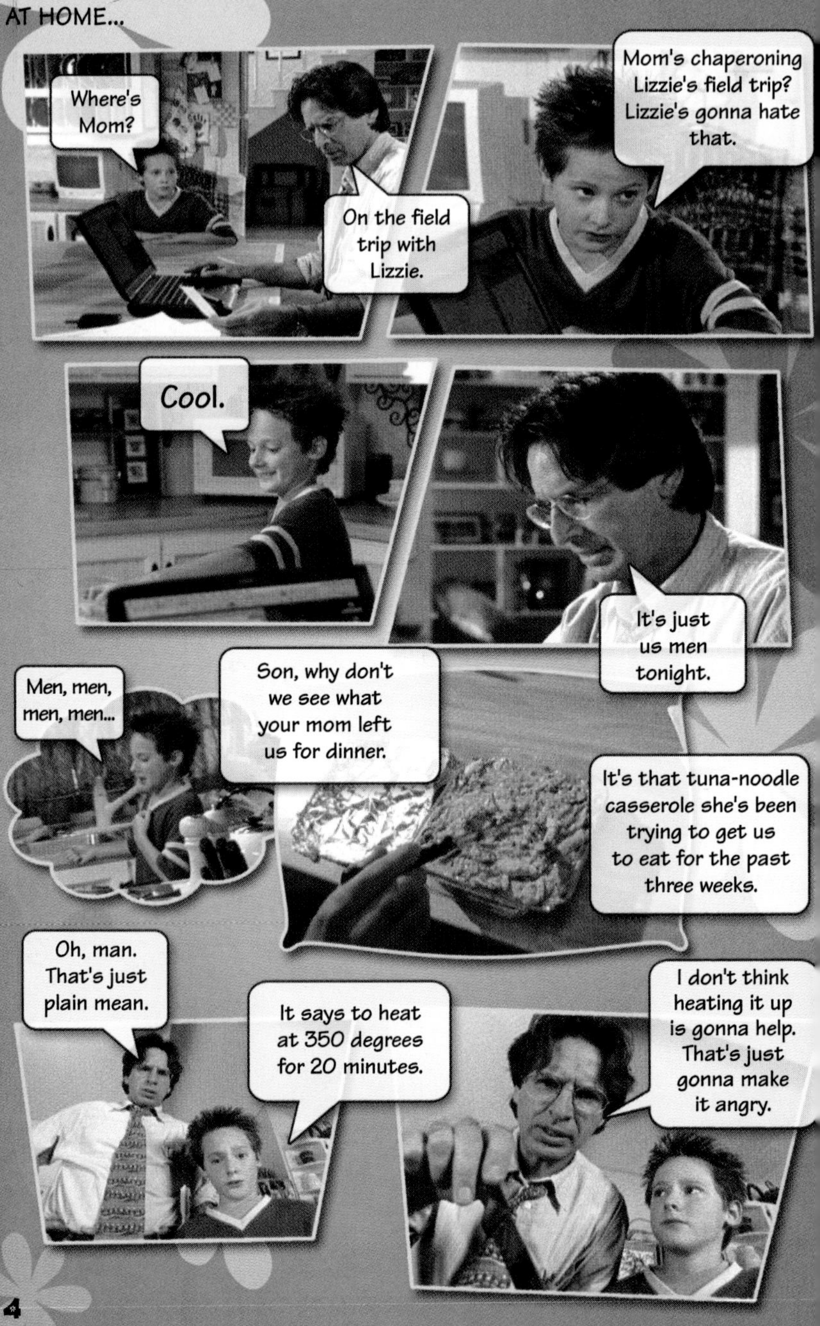
AT HOME...
Where's Mom?
On the field trip with Lizzie.
Mom's chaperoning Lizzie's field trip? Lizzie's gonna hate that.
Cool.
It's just us men tonight.
Men, men, men, men...
Son, why don't we see what your mom left us for dinner.
It's that tuna-noodle casserole she's been trying to get us to eat for the past three weeks.
Oh, man. That's just plain mean.
It says to heat at 350 degrees for 20 minutes.
I don't think heating it up is gonna help. That's just gonna make it angry.

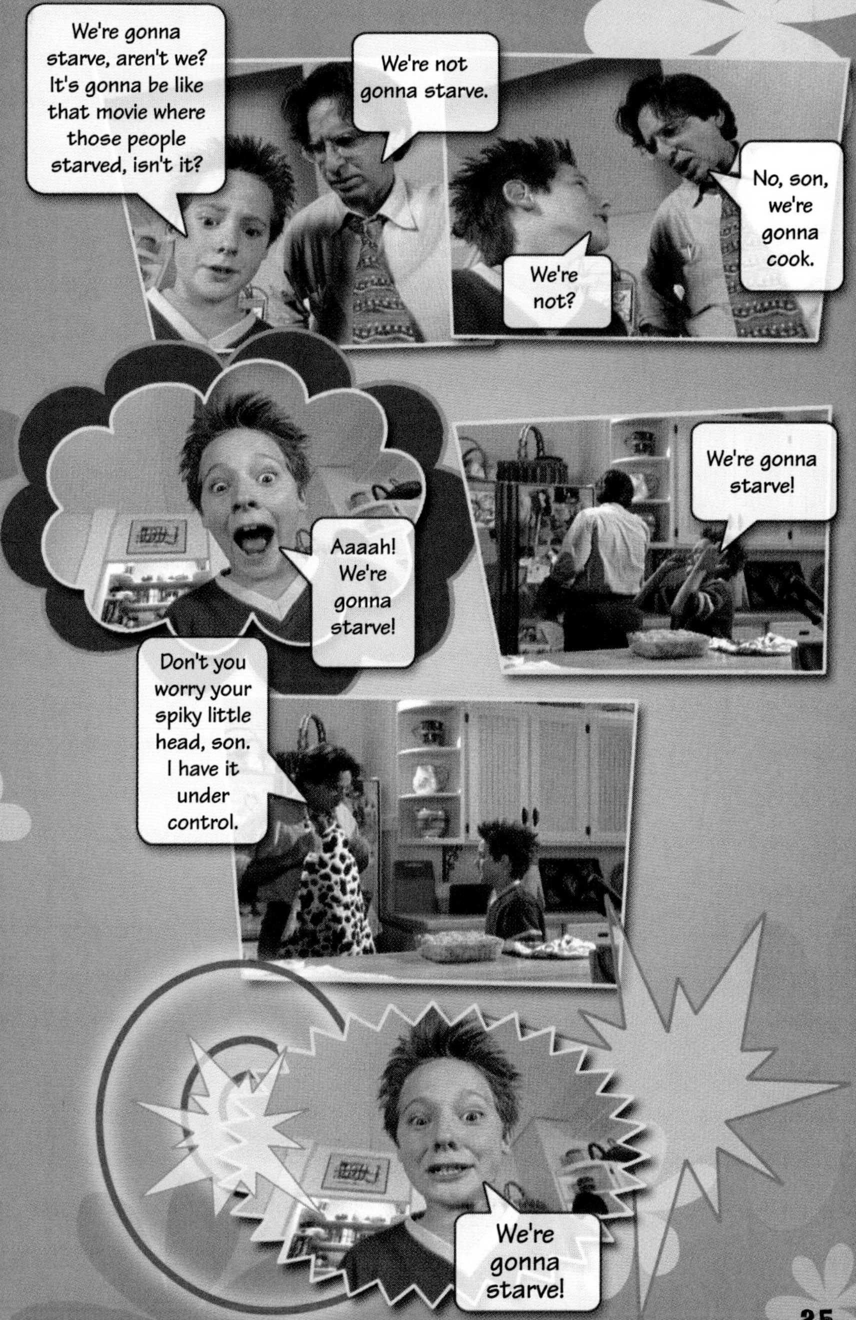
We're gonna starve, aren't we? It's gonna be like that movie where those people starved, isn't it?
We're not gonna starve.
We're not?
No, son, we're gonna cook.
Aaaah! We're gonna starve!
We're gonna starve!
Don't you worry your spiky little head, son. I have it under control.
We're gonna starve!

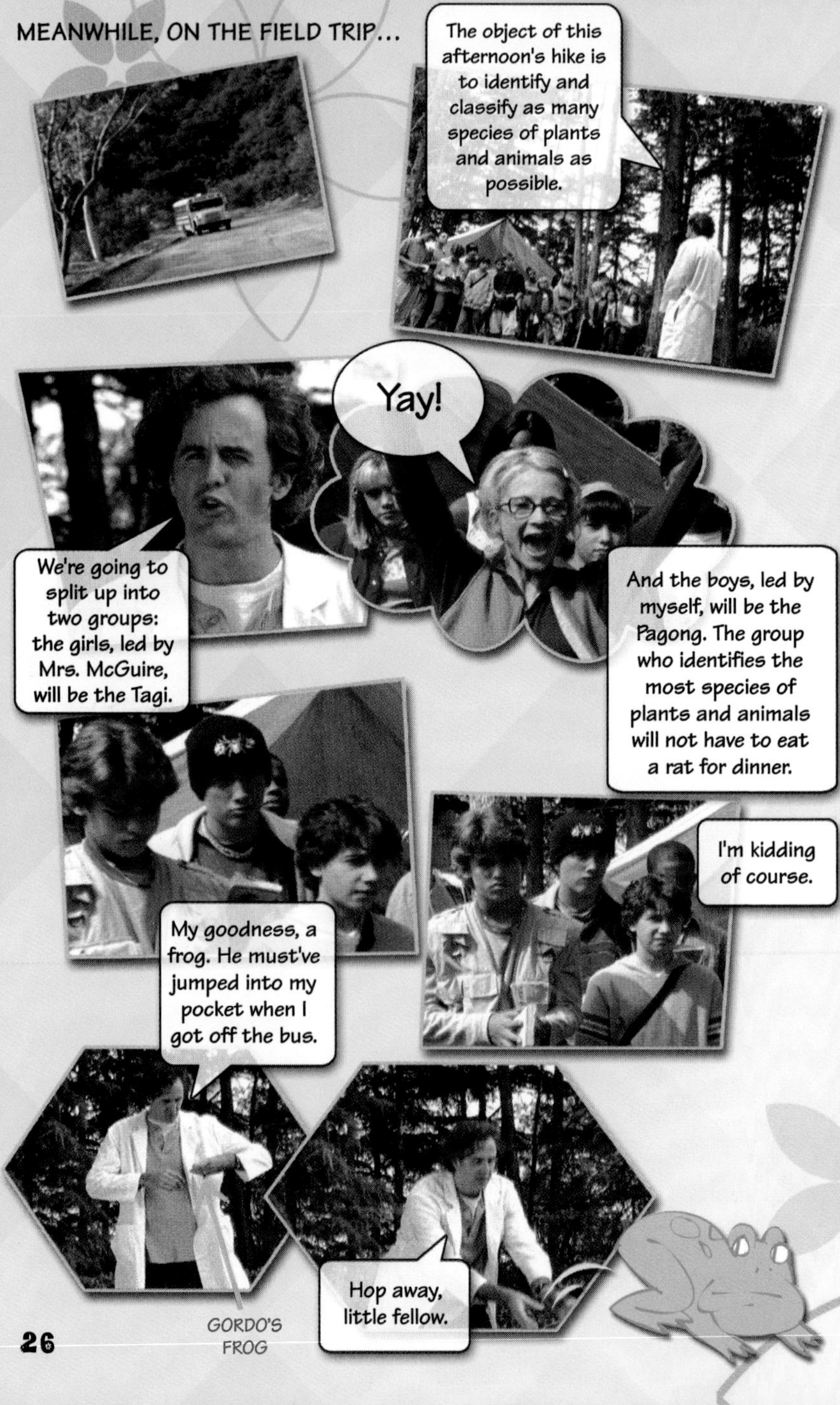
MEANWHILE, ON THE FIELD TRIP...
The object of this afternoon's hike is to identify and classify as many species of plants and animals as possible.
We're going to split up into two groups: the girls, led by Mrs. McGuire, will be the Tagi.
Yay!
And the boys, led by myself, will be the Pagong. The group who identifies the most species of plants and animals will not have to eat a rat for dinner.
I'm kidding of course.
My goodness, a frog. He must've jumped into my pocket when I got off the bus.
Hop away, little fellow.
GORDO'S FROG

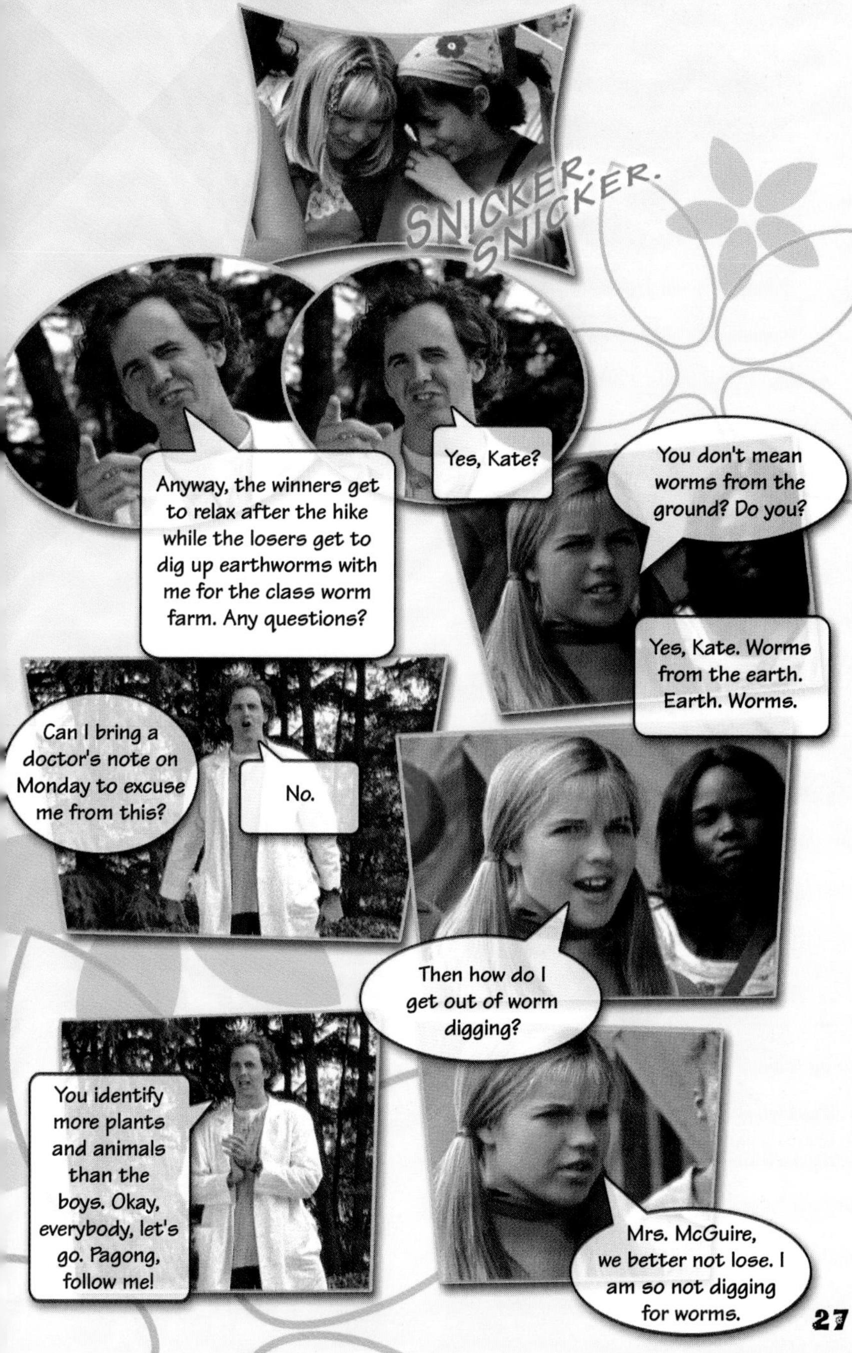
SNICKER. SNICKER.
Anyway, the winners get to relax after the hike while the losers get to dig up earthworms with me for the class worm farm. Any questions?
Yes, Kate?
You don't mean worms from the ground? Do you?
Yes, Kate. Worms from the earth. Earth. Worms.
Can I bring a doctor's note on Monday to excuse me from this?
No.
Then how do I get out of worm digging?
You identify more plants and animals than the boys. Okay, everybody, let's go. Pagong, follow me!
Mrs. McGuire, we better not lose. I am so not digging for worms.

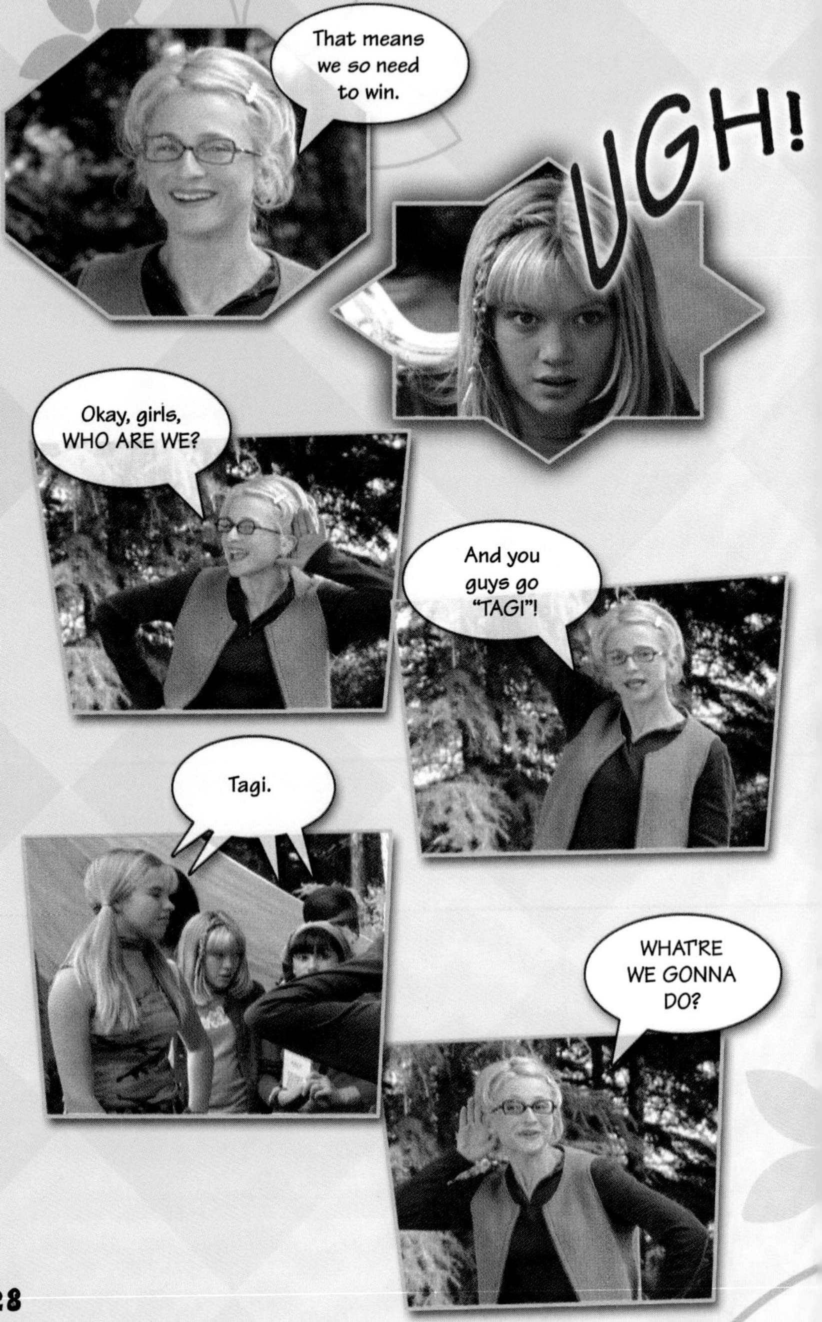
That means we so need to win.
UGH!
Okay, girls, WHO ARE WE?
And you guys go "TAGI"!
Tagi.
WHAT'RE WE GONNA DO?

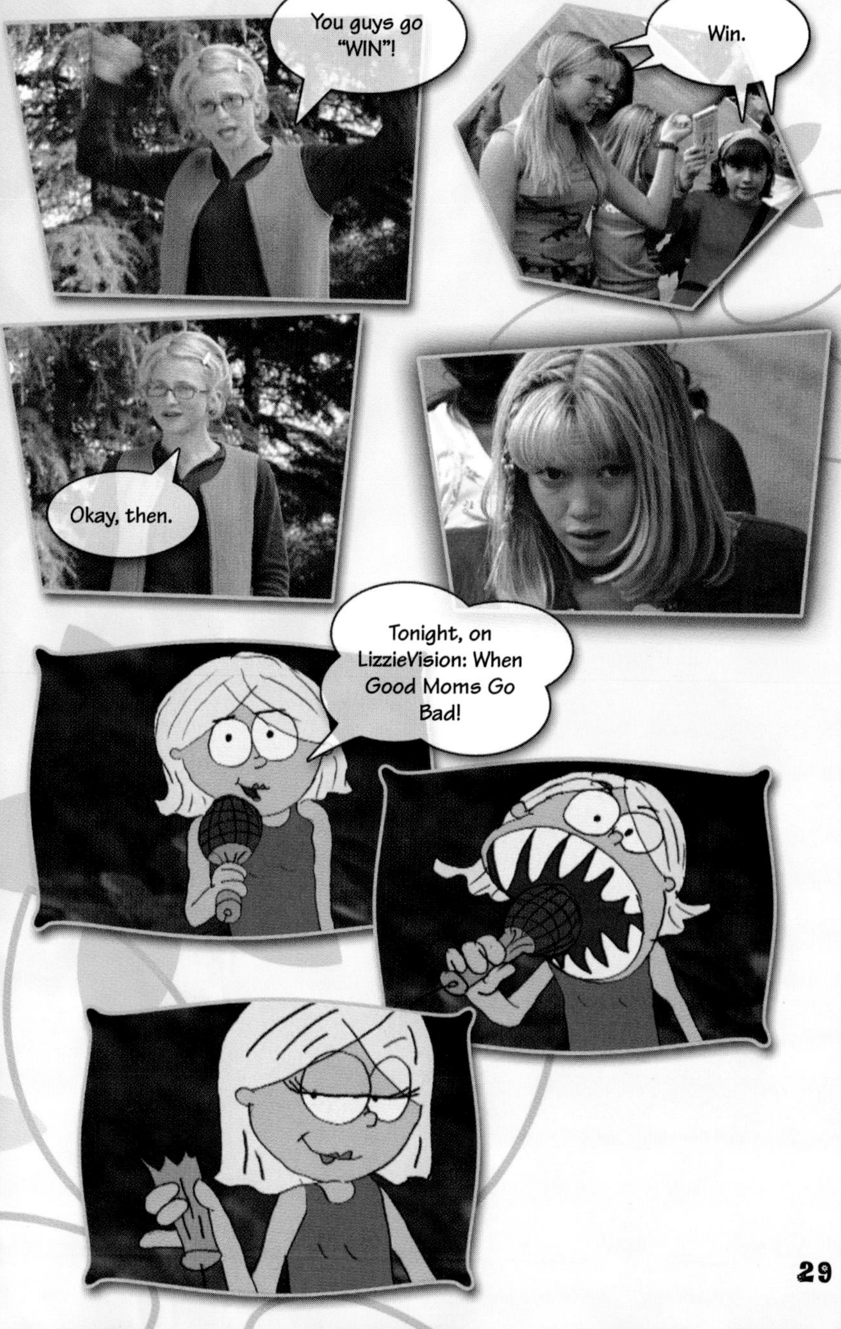
You guys go "WIN"!
Win.
Okay, then.
Tonight, on LizzieVision: When Good Moms Go Bad!

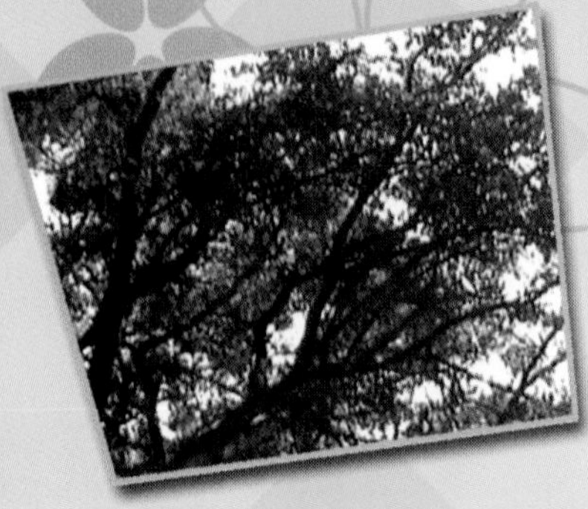

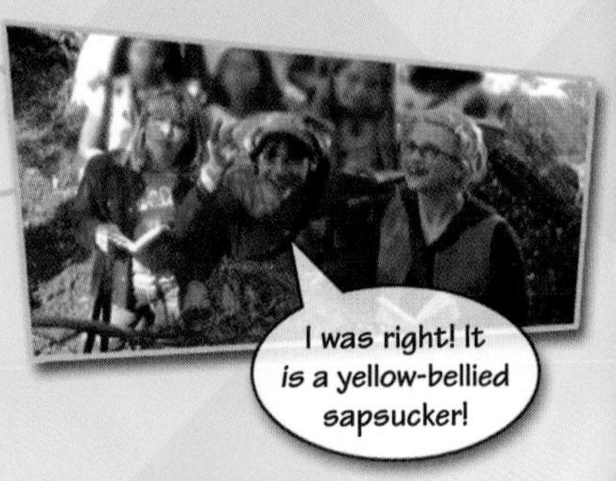
I was right! It is a yellow-bellied sapsucker!

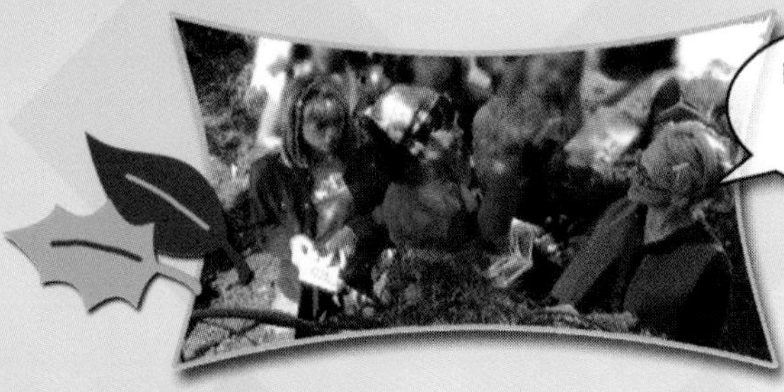
Excellent job! High five, girlfriend!

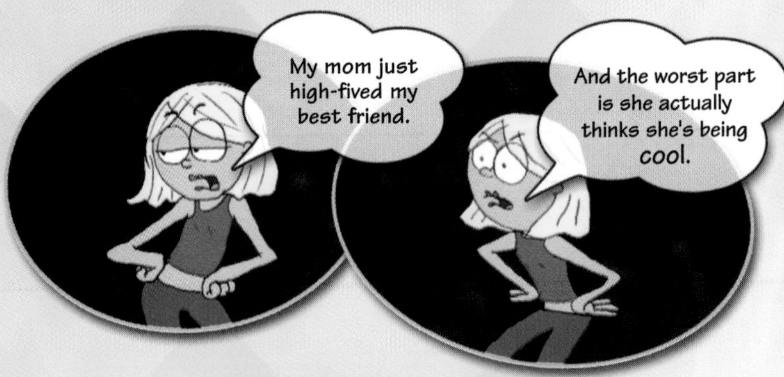
My mom just high-fived my best friend.
And the worst part is she actually thinks she's being cool.

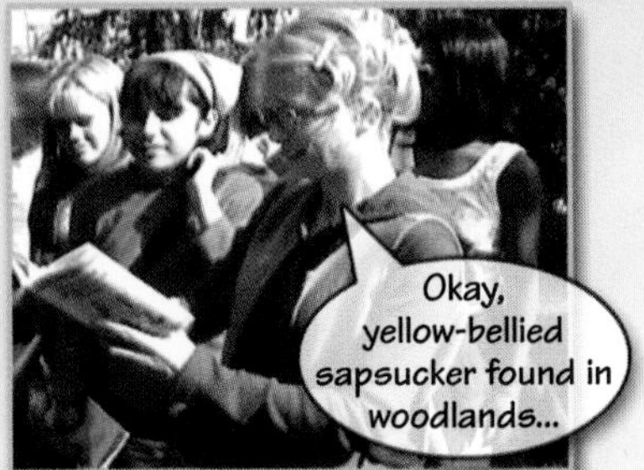
Okay, yellow-bellied sapsucker found in woodlands...

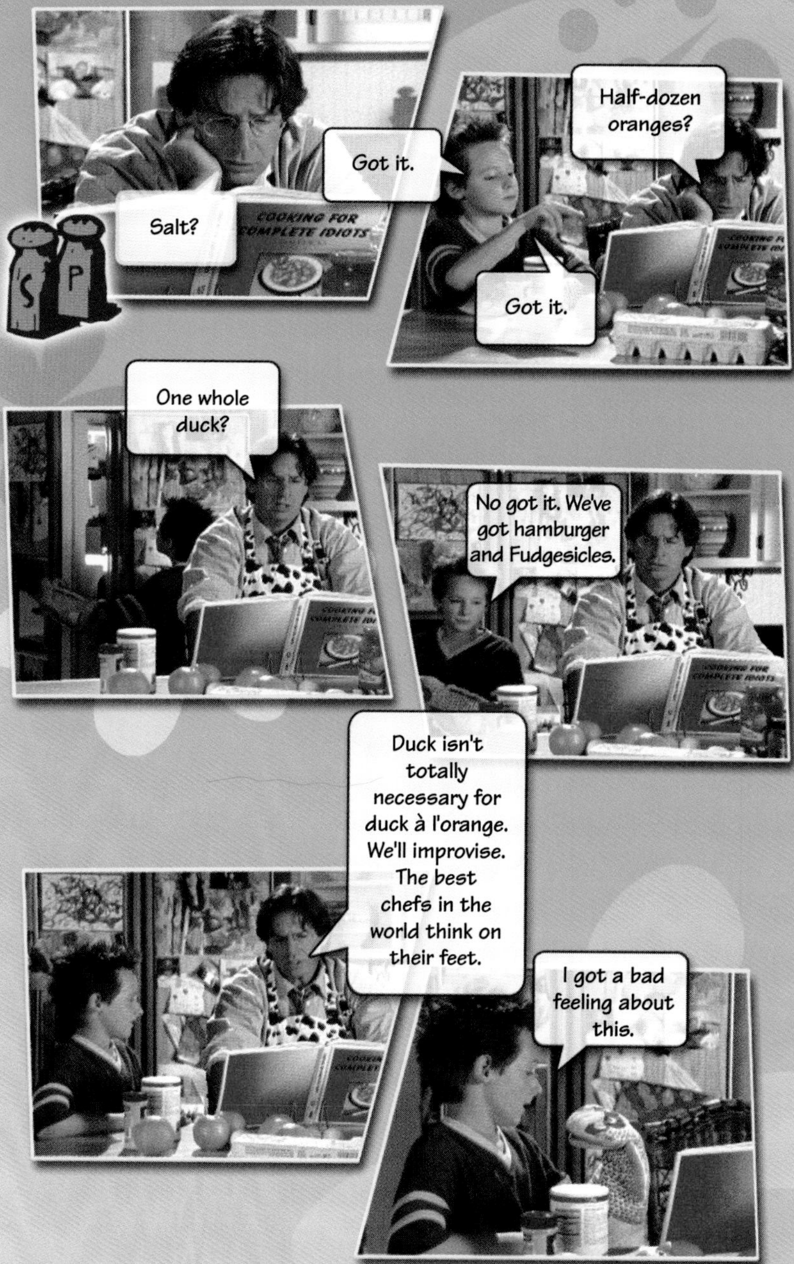
Salt?
Got it.
Half-dozen oranges?
Got it.
One whole duck?
No got it. We've got hamburger and Fudgesicles.
Duck isn't totally necessary for duck à l'orange. We'll improvise. The best chefs in the world think on their feet.
I got a bad feeling about this.

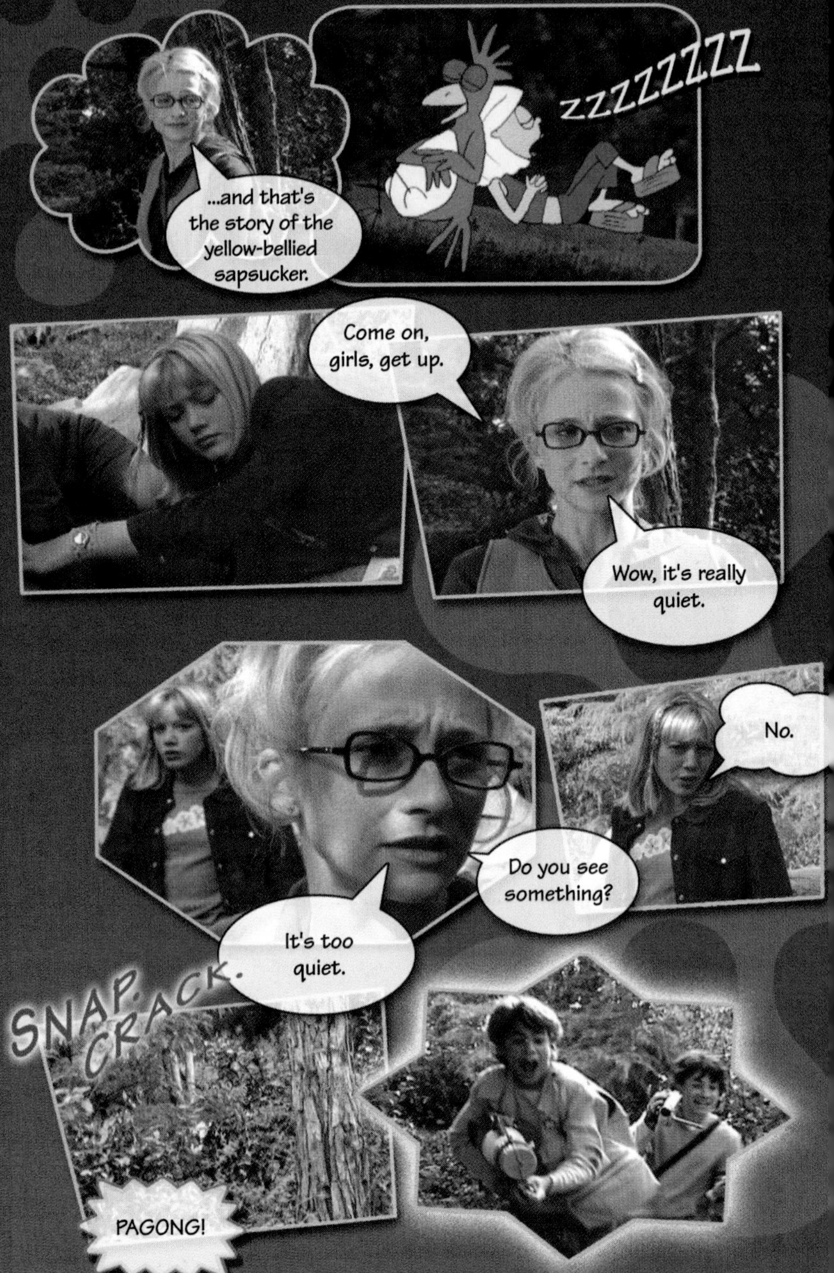
...and that's the story of the yellow-bellied sapsucker.
ZZZZZZZZ
Come on, girls, get up.
Wow, it's really quiet.
Do you see something?
It's too quiet.
No.
SNAP. CRACK.
PAGONG!

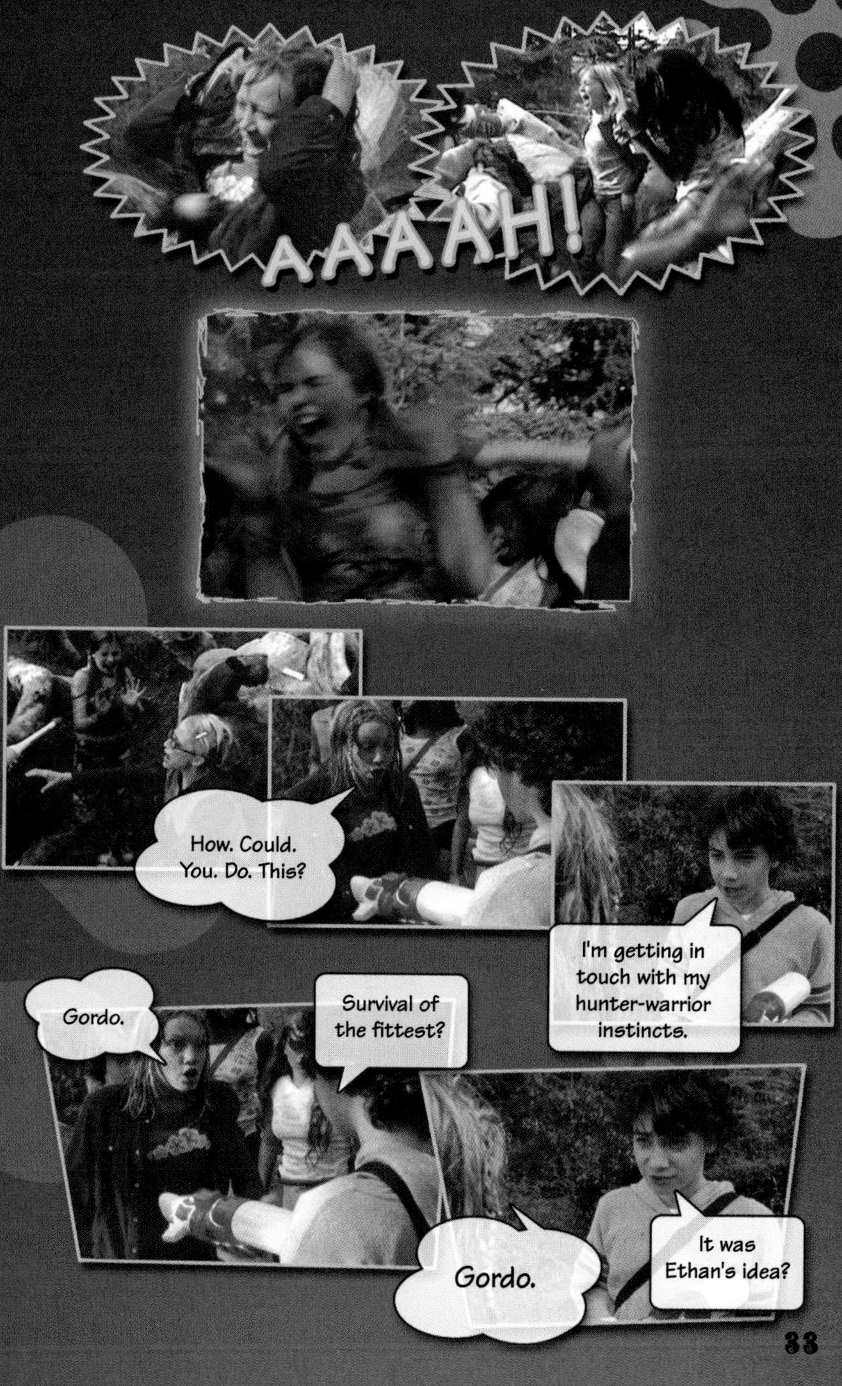
AAAAH!
How. Could. You. Do. This?
I'm getting in touch with my hunter-warrior instincts.
Gordo.
Survival of the fittest?
Gordo.
It was Ethan's idea?

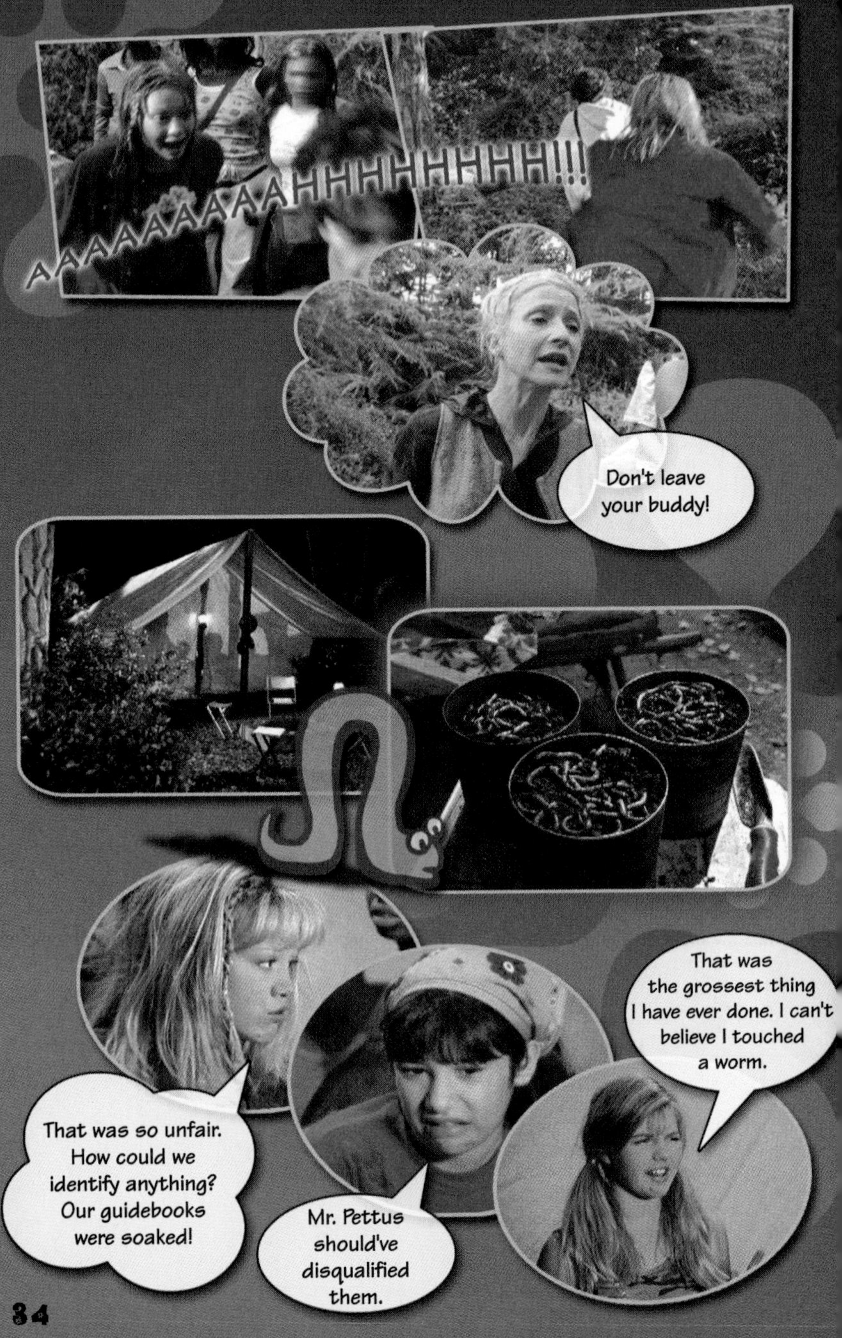
AAAAAAAAAAHHHHHHHHHH!!!
Don't leave your buddy!
That was so unfair. How could we identify anything? Our guidebooks were soaked!
Mr. Pettus should've disqualified them.
That was the grossest thing I have ever done. I can't believe I touched a worm.

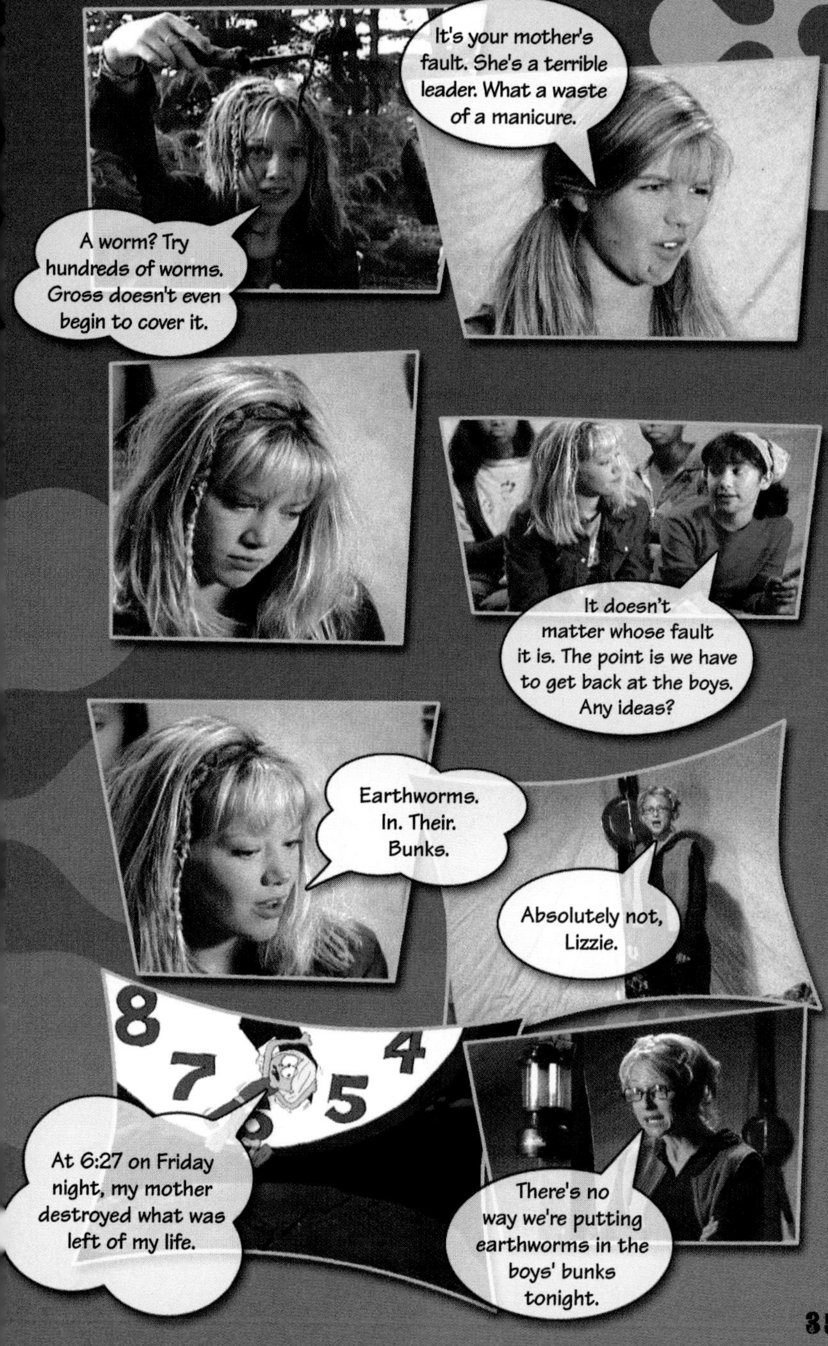
A worm? Try hundreds of worms. Gross doesn't even begin to cover it.
It's your mother's fault. She's a terrible leader. What a waste of a manicure.
It doesn't matter whose fault it is. The point is we have to get back at the boys. Any ideas?
Earthworms. In. Their. Bunks.
Absolutely not, Lizzie.
8
7
6
5
4
At 6:27 on Friday night, my mother destroyed what was left of my life.
There's no way we're putting earthworms in the boys' bunks tonight.

Forget the boys. Mom's getting earthworms in her bunk tonight.
Oh yeah. Someone's gonna have to take them in there. Do we really want to touch the worms again?
Forget it. Besides, boys like earthworms.
But we have to get them back. The only thing we have more of than earthworms is toilet paper. Maybe we should fill their bunks with toilet paper.
Now that is a great idea.
Huh?
Huh?
Huh?

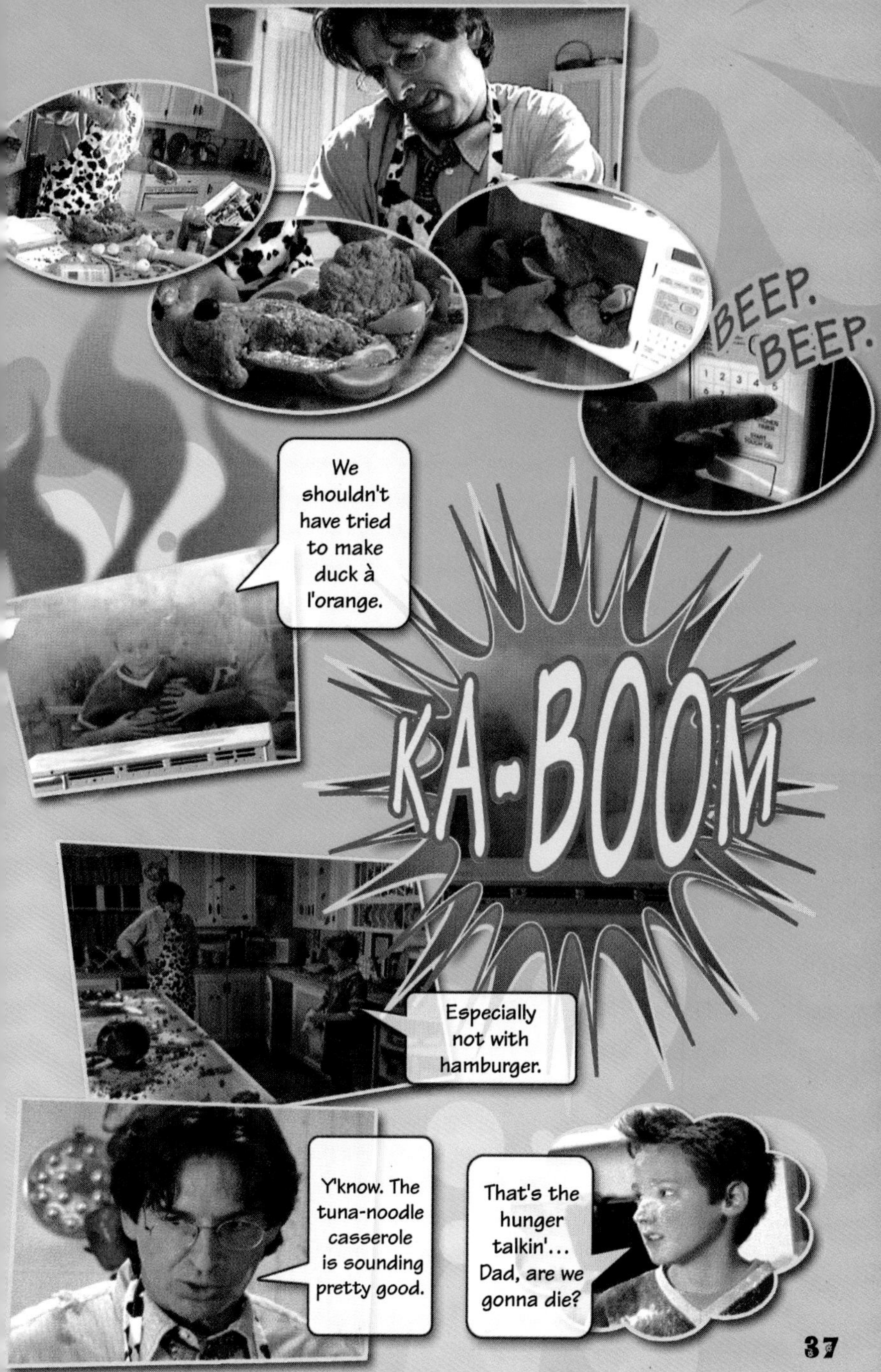
BEEP. BEEP.
We shouldn't have tried to make duck à l'orange.
KA-BOOM
Especially not with hamburger.
Y'know. The tuna-noodle casserole is sounding pretty good.
That's the hunger talkin'... Dad, are we gonna die?

Okay, c'mon. Now this is fun.
You wouldn't be saying that if it was your mom.
Okay, this is it.
My mom wouldn't lead a midnight T.P. raid on the boys' tent.
Mrs. McGuire, are you gonna get us into more trouble?
Yes, it may get you in trouble. Stay in the tent, and let the boys have their victory. Stay in the tent, and you may not get detention. Or you can follow me and T.P.
Here. Do your war paint.
No! Are you kidding? Stop encouraging her.

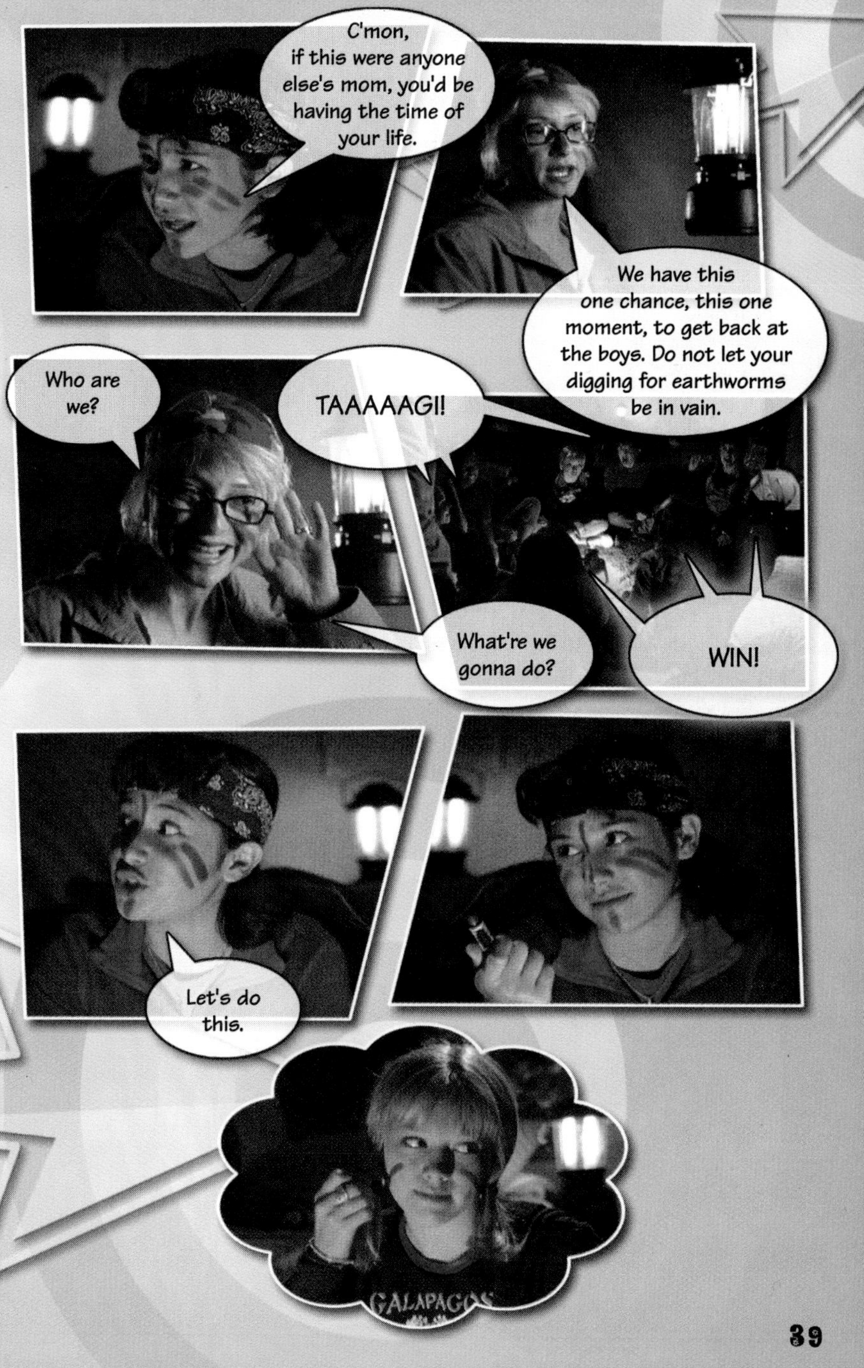
C'mon, if this were anyone else's mom, you'd be having the time of your life.
We have this one chance, this one moment, to get back at the boys. Do not let your digging for earthworms be in vain.
Who are we?
TAAAAAGI!
What're we gonna do?
WIN!
Let's do this.
GALAPAGOS

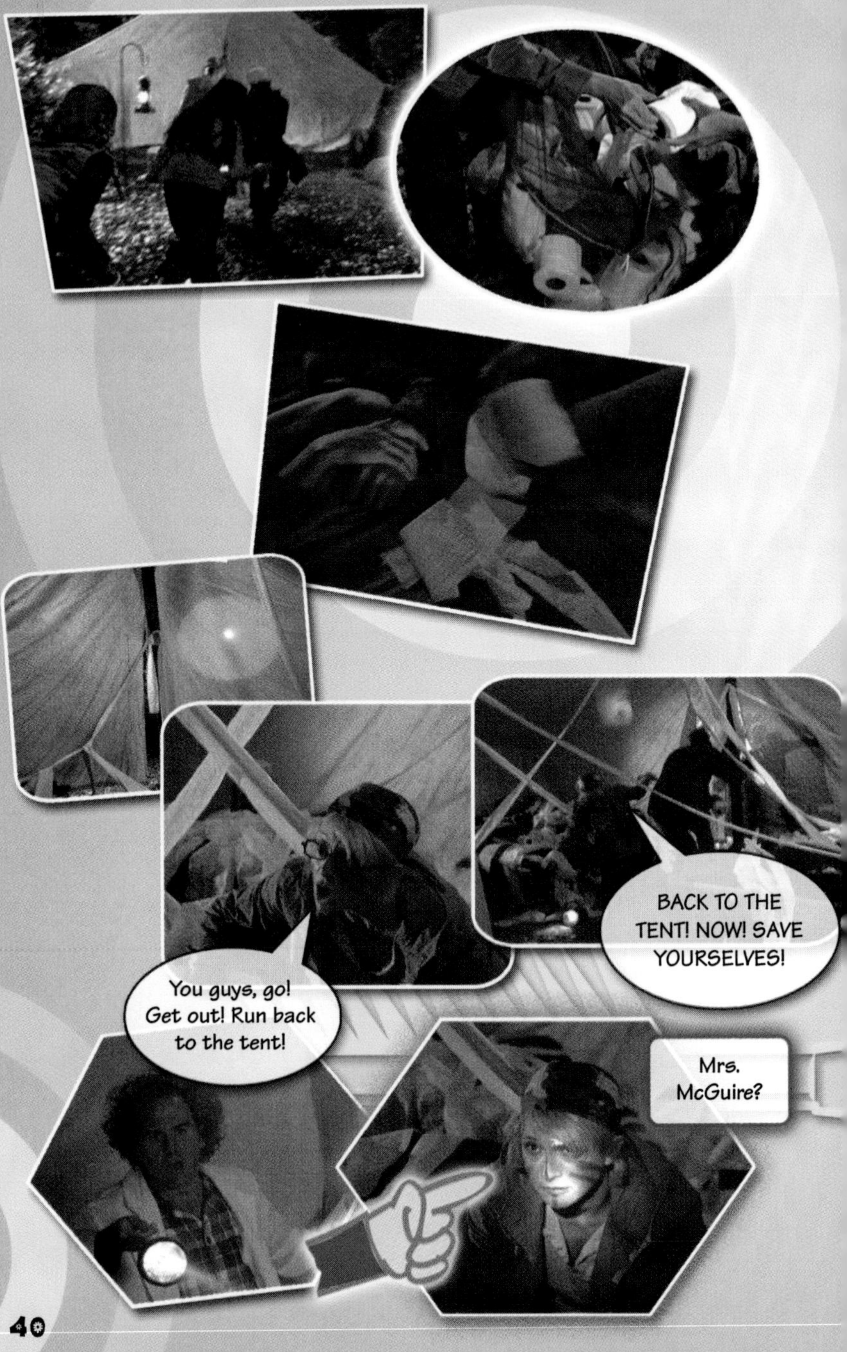
You guys, go! Get out! Run back to the tent!
BACK TO THE TENT! NOW! SAVE YOURSELVES!
Mrs. McGuire?

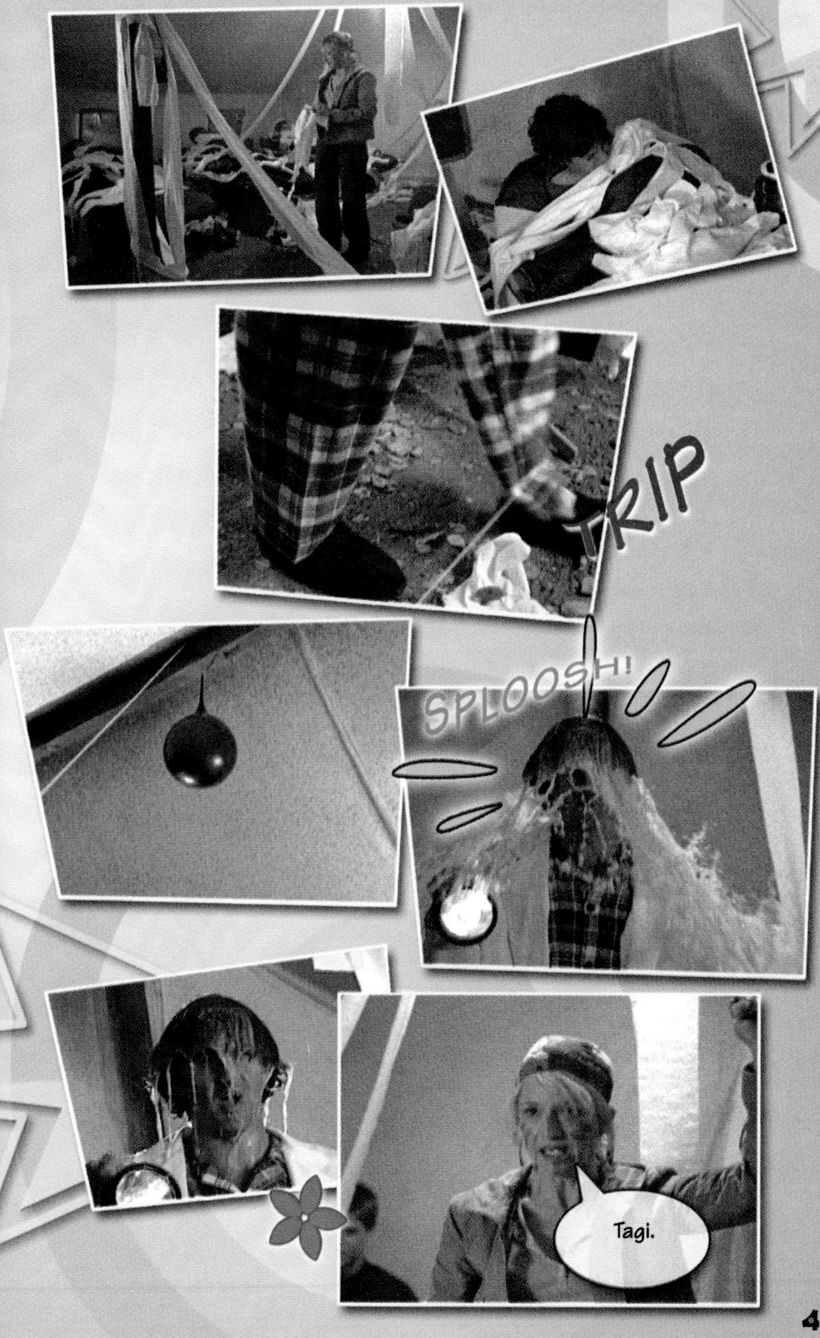
TRIP
SPLOOSH!
Tagi.

MEANWHILE, AT HOME...

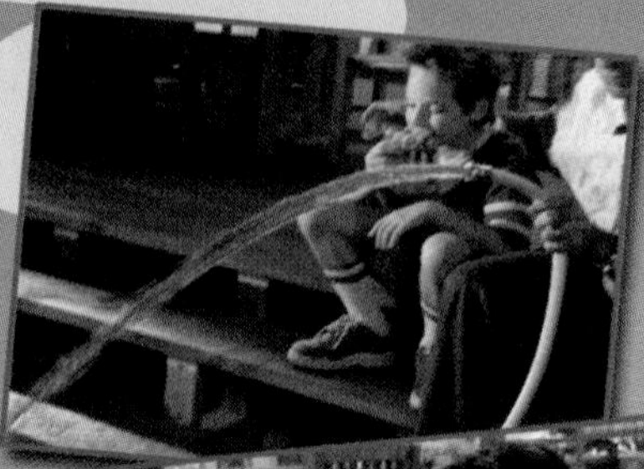

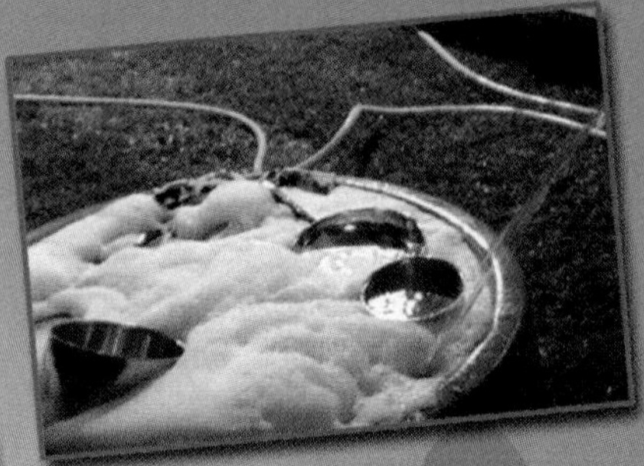

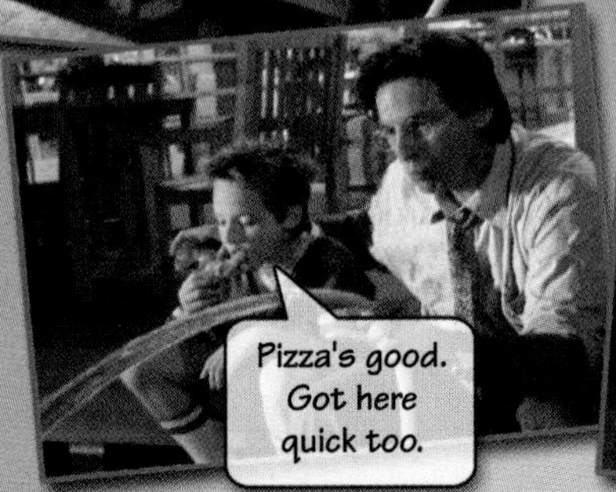
Pizza's good. Got here quick too.

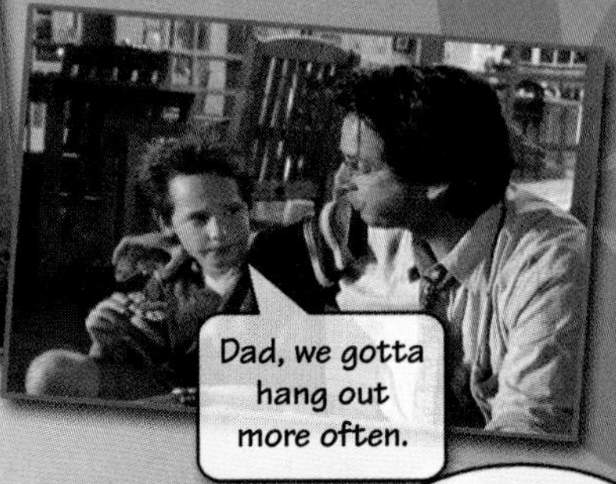
Dad, we gotta hang out more often.

THE NEXT MORNING...

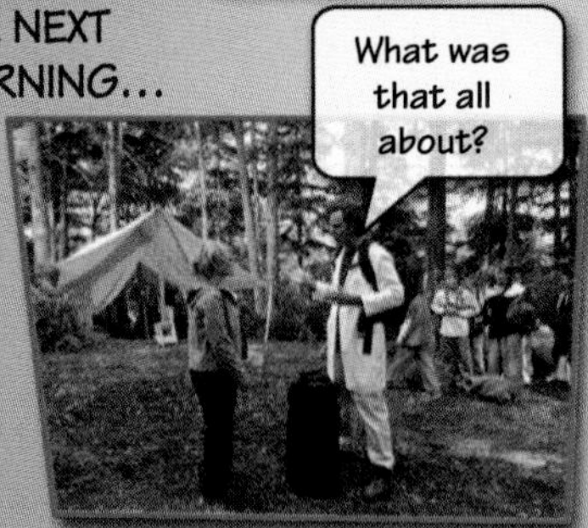
What was that all about?

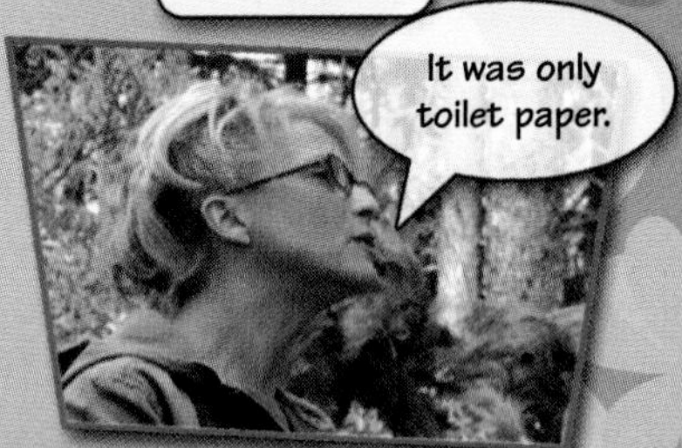
It was only toilet paper.

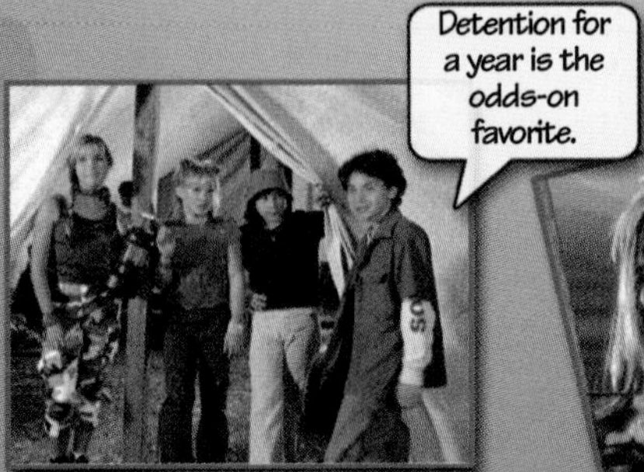
Detention for a year is the odds-on favorite.

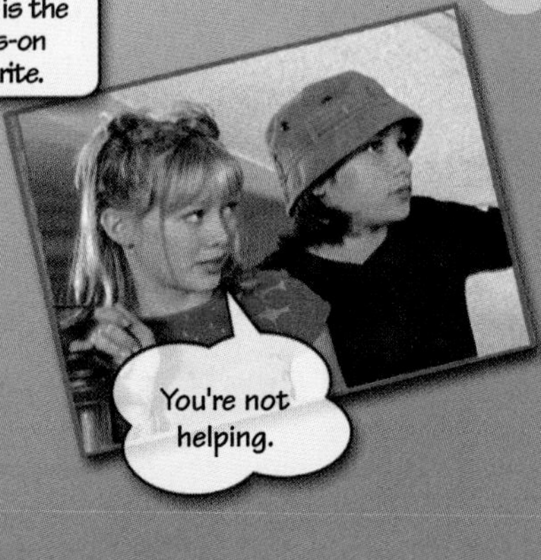
You're not helping.

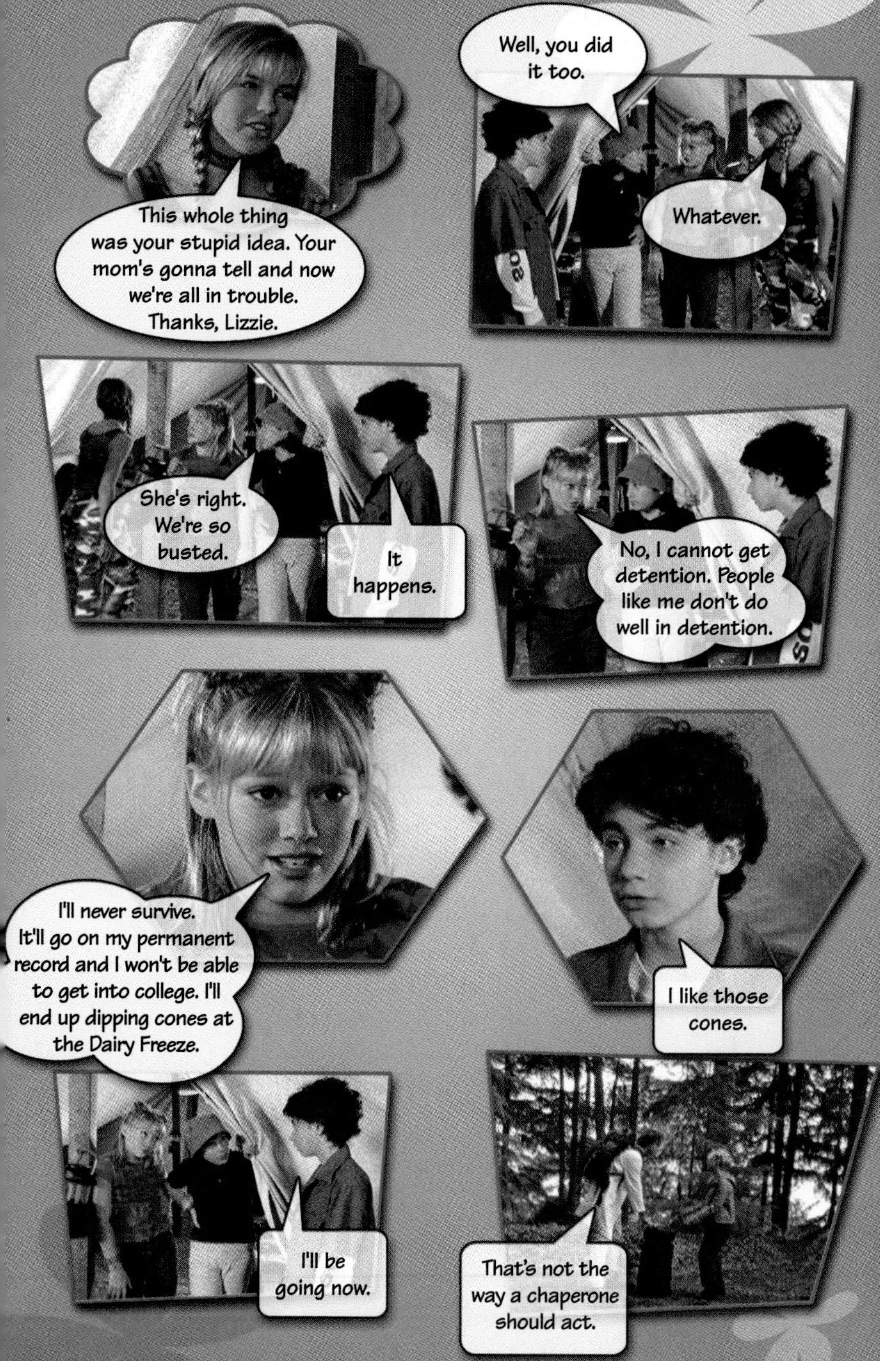
This whole thing was your stupid idea. Your mom's gonna tell and now we're all in trouble. Thanks, Lizzie.
Well, you did it too.
Whatever.
She's right. We're so busted.
It happens.
No, I cannot get detention. People like me don't do well in detention.
I'll never survive. It'll go on my permanent record and I won't be able to get into college. I'll end up dipping cones at the Dairy Freeze.
I like those cones.
I'll be going now.
That's not the way a chaperone should act.

INSIDE THE GIRLS' TENT...

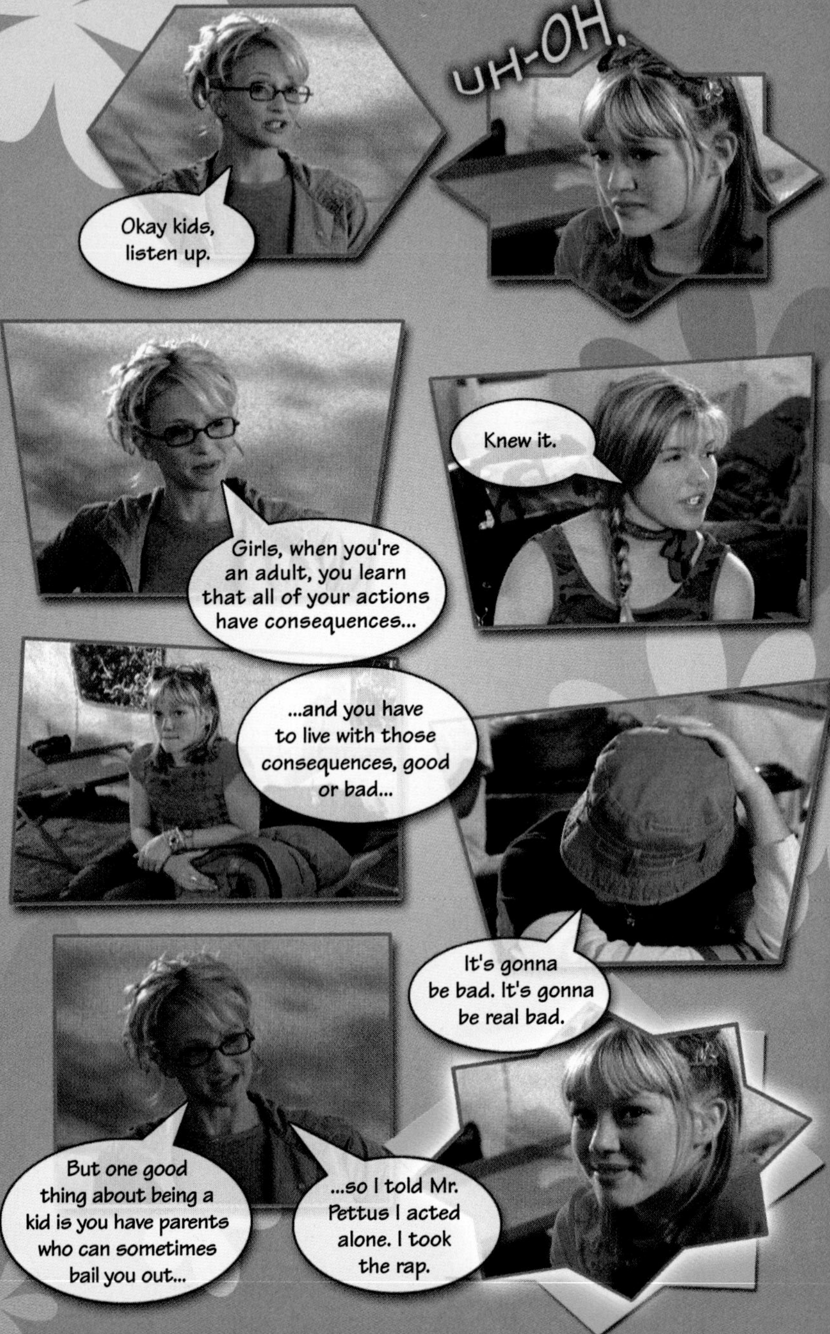
Okay kids, listen up.
UH-OH.
Girls, when you're an adult, you learn that all of your actions have consequences...
Knew it.
...and you have to live with those consequences, good or bad...
It's gonna be bad. It's gonna be real bad.
But one good thing about being a kid is you have parents who can sometimes bail you out...
...so I told Mr. Pettus I acted alone. I took the rap.

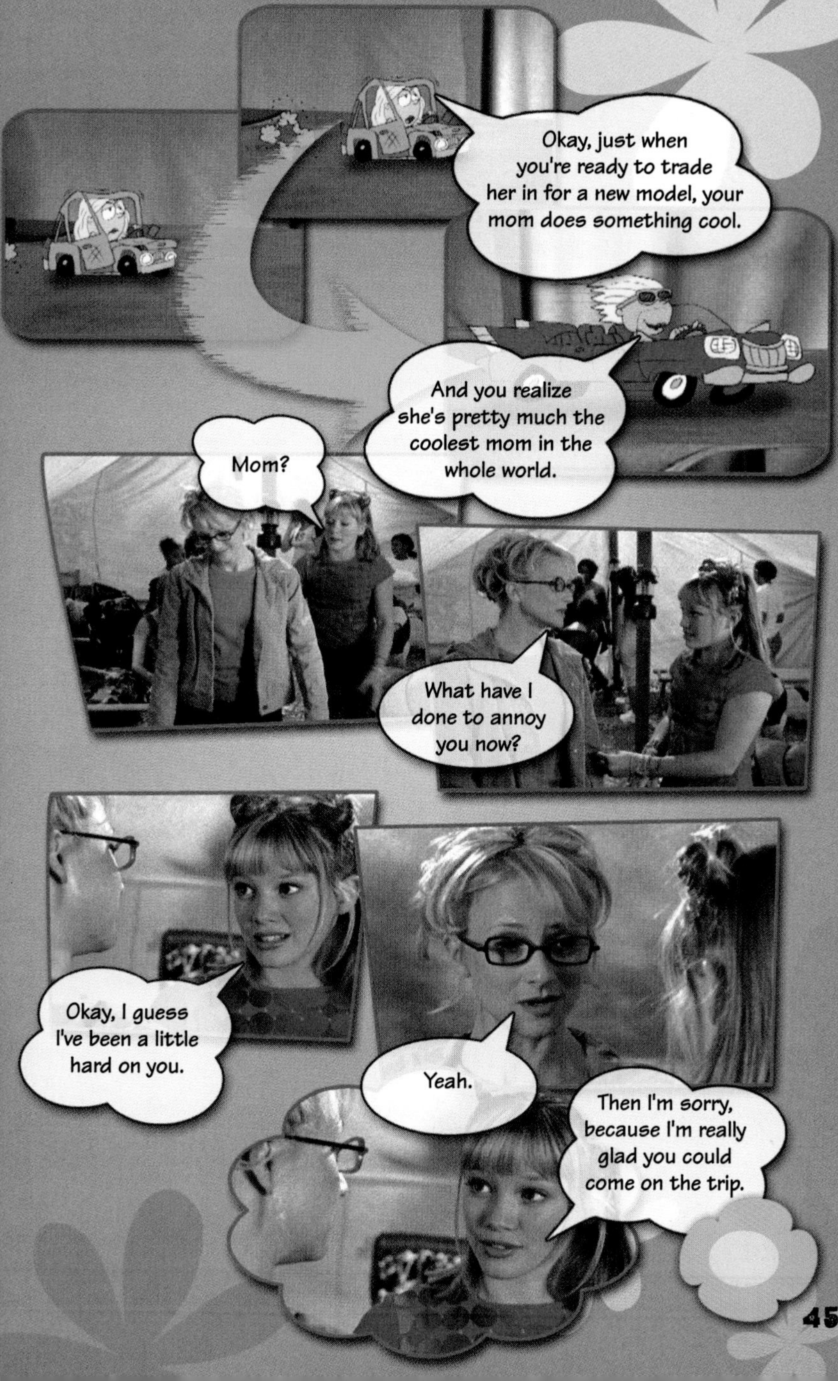

Okay, just when you're ready to trade her in for a new model, your mom does something cool.
And you realize she's pretty much the coolest mom in the whole world.
Mom?
What have I done to annoy you now?
Okay, I guess I've been a little hard on you.
Yeah.
Then I'm sorry, because I'm really glad you could come on the trip.

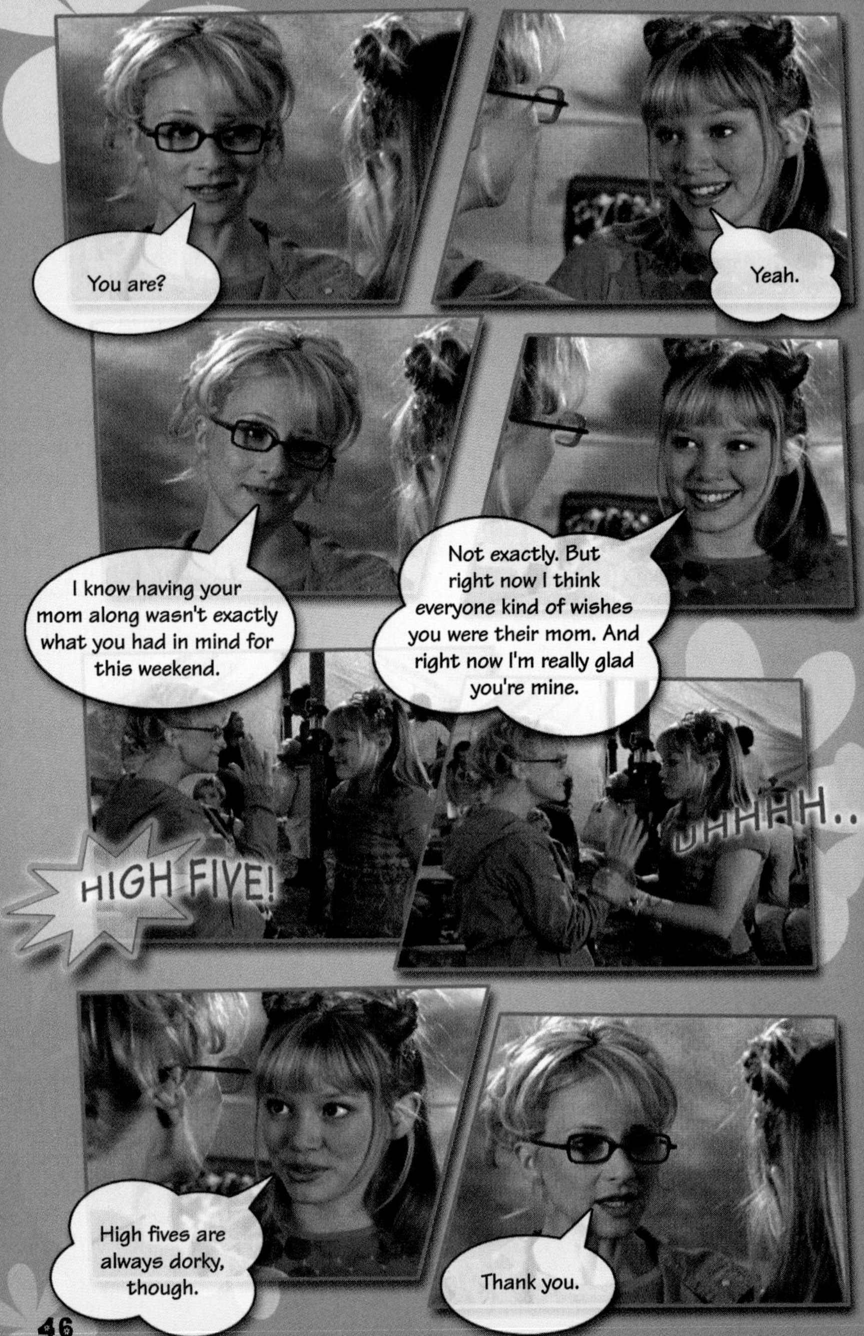
You are?
Yeah.
I know having your mom along wasn't exactly what you had in mind for this weekend.
Not exactly. But right now I think everyone kind of wishes you were their mom. And right now I'm really glad you're mine.
HIGH FIVE!
UHHHH..
High fives are always dorky, though.
Thank you.

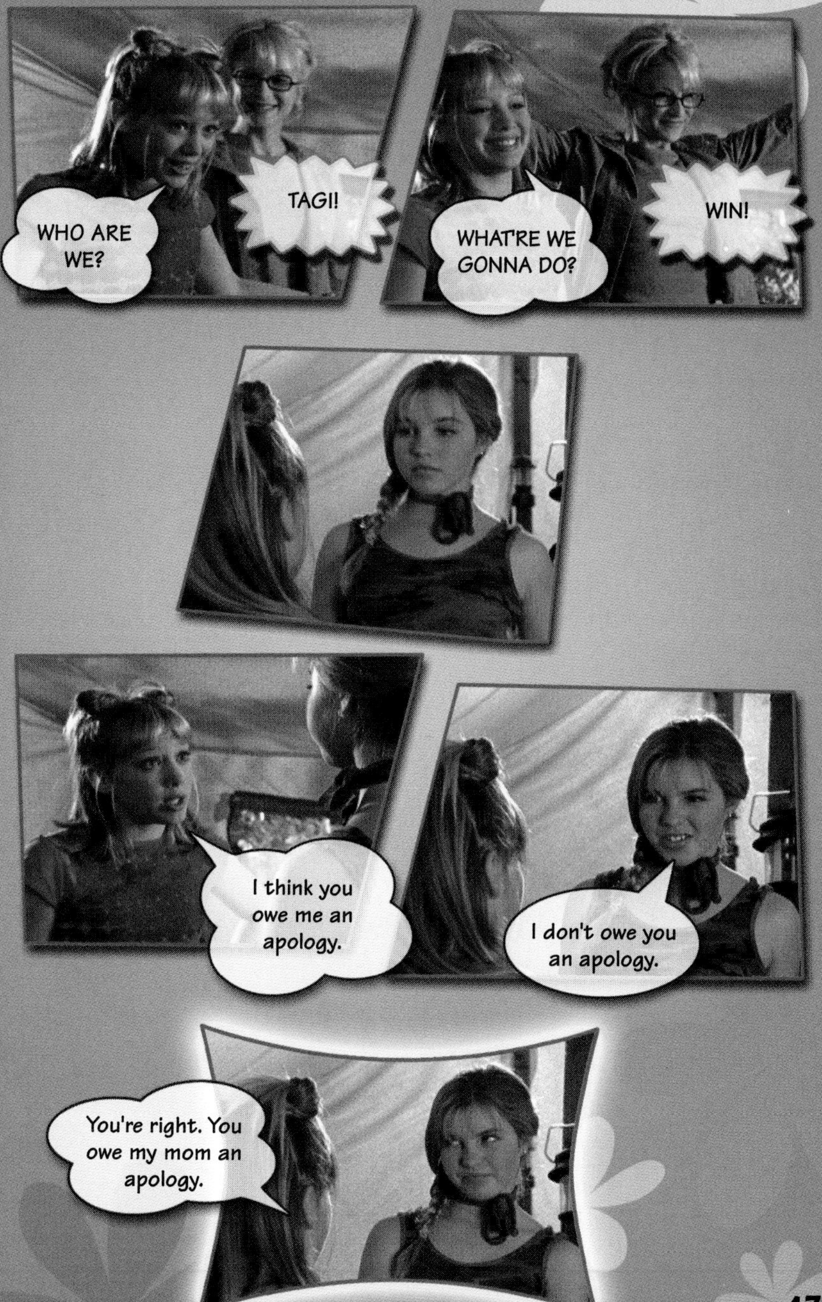
WHO ARE WE?
TAGI!
WHAT'RE WE GONNA DO?
WIN!
I think you owe me an apology.
I don't owe you an apology.
You're right. You owe my mom an apology.

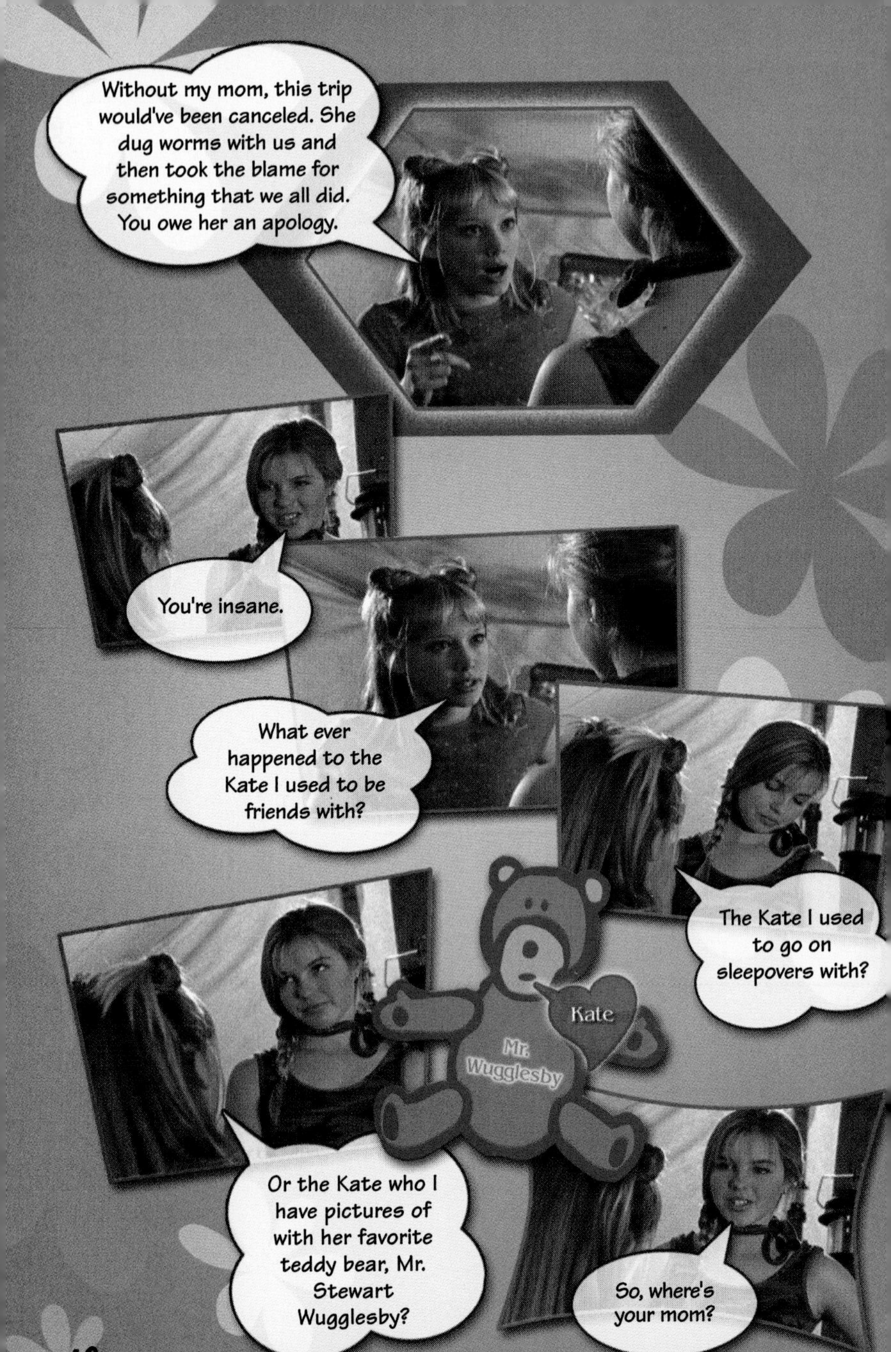

Without my mom, this trip would've been canceled. She dug worms with us and then took the blame for something that we all did. You owe her an apology.
You're insane.
What ever happened to the Kate I used to be friends with?
The Kate I used to go on sleepovers with?
Mr. Wugglesby
Kate
Or the Kate who I have pictures of with her favorite teddy bear, Mr. Stewart Wugglesby?
So, where's your mom?

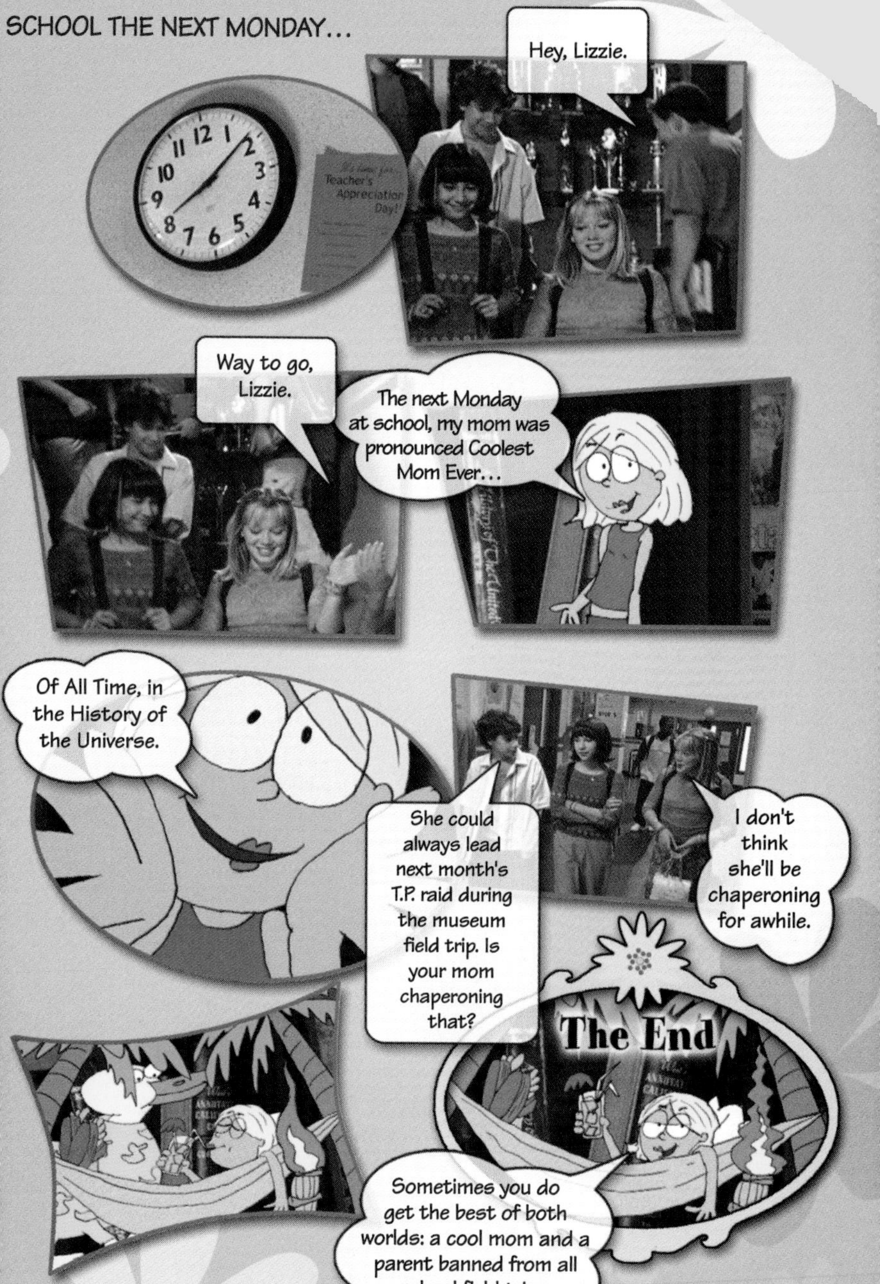
SCHOOL THE NEXT MONDAY…
Teacher's Appreciation Day!
Hey, Lizzie.
Way to go, Lizzie.
The next Monday at school, my mom was pronounced Coolest Mom Ever…
Of All Time, in the History of the Universe.
She could always lead next month's T.P. raid during the museum field trip. Is your mom chaperoning that?
I don't think she'll be chaperoning for awhile.
The End
Sometimes you do get the best of both worlds: a cool mom and a parent banned from all school field trips.

Lizzie McGuire

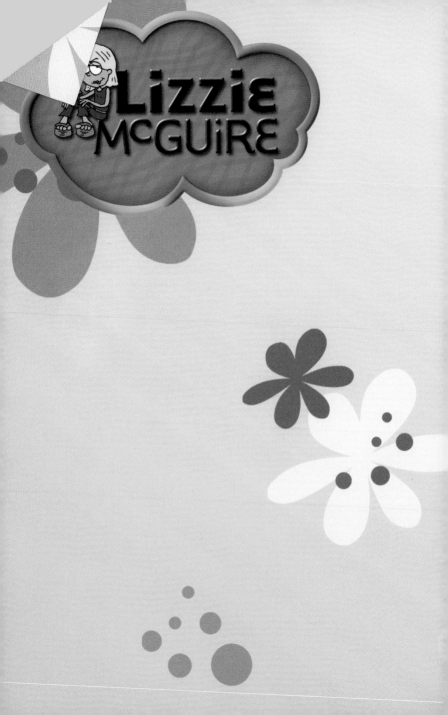

Episode 6

"Misadventures in Babysitting"

When the babysitter cancels, Lizzie convinces her parents that she's old enough to take on the job. She doesn't count on Matt being a "super brat" or Gordo and Miranda being mad at her or— the burglar!

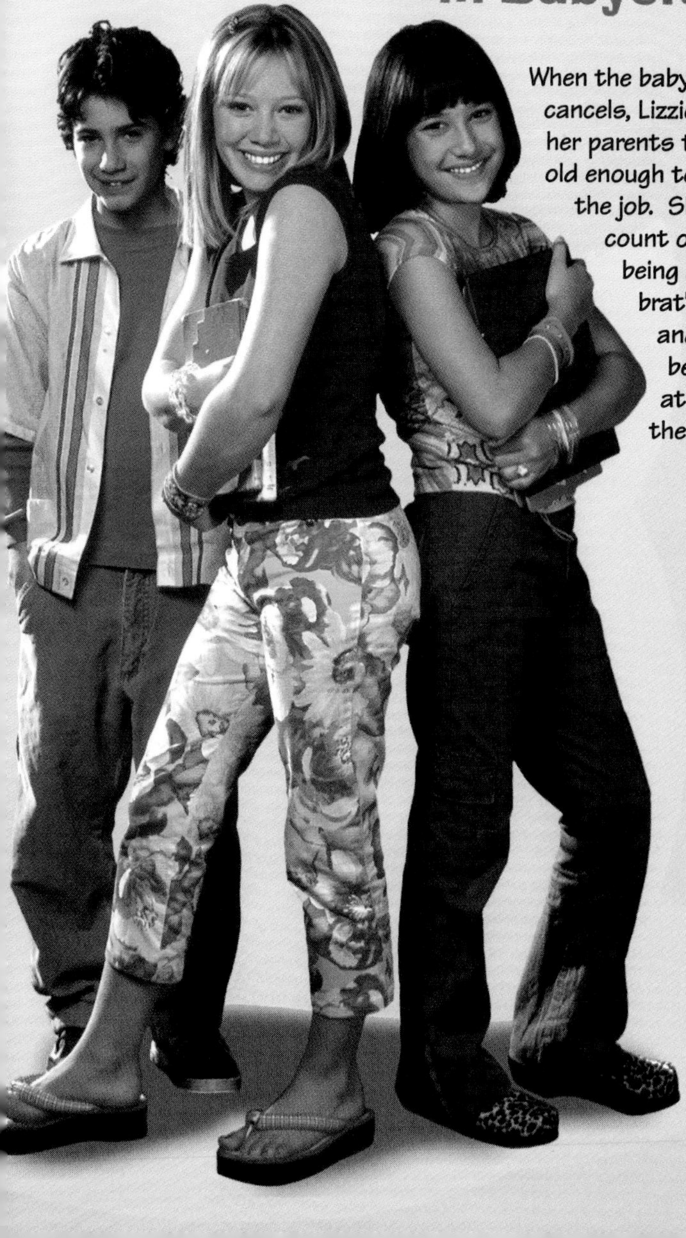

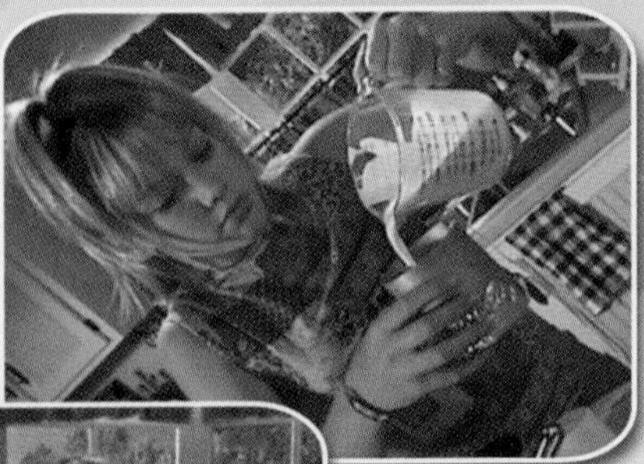

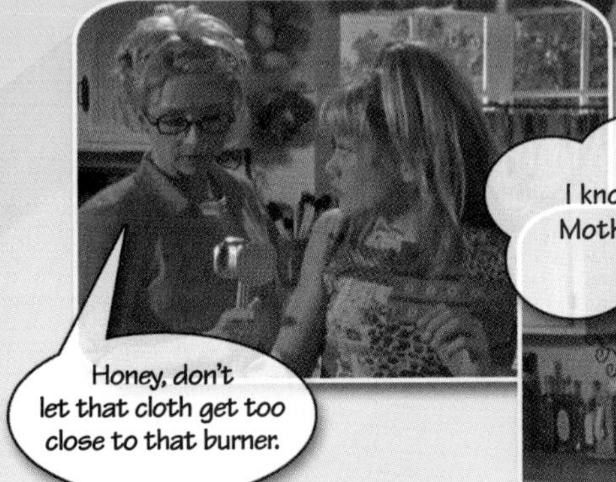

Honey, don't let that cloth get too close to that burner.

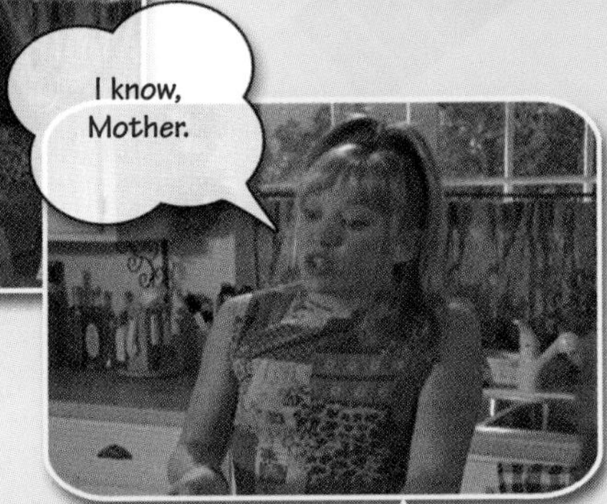

I know, Mother.

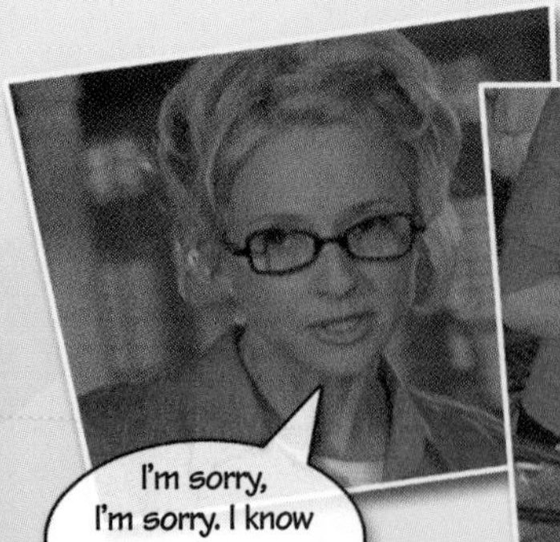

I'm sorry, I'm sorry. I know you're not a small child.

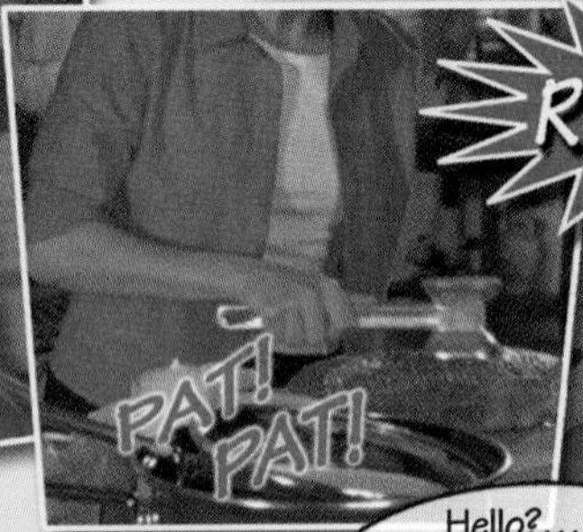

PAT! PAT!

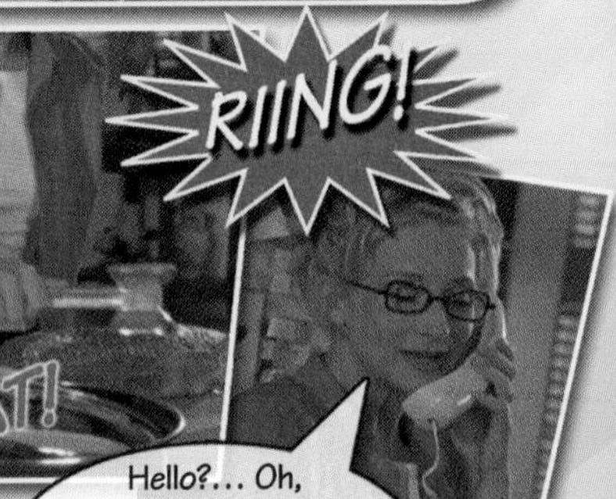

RIING!
Hello?... Oh, hey, Debby... Well, if you can't baby-sit tomorrow night, you can't baby-sit.

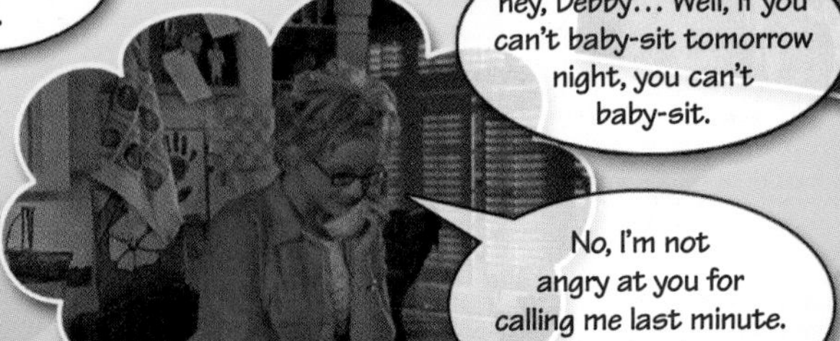

No, I'm not angry at you for calling me last minute. Okay, bye-bye.

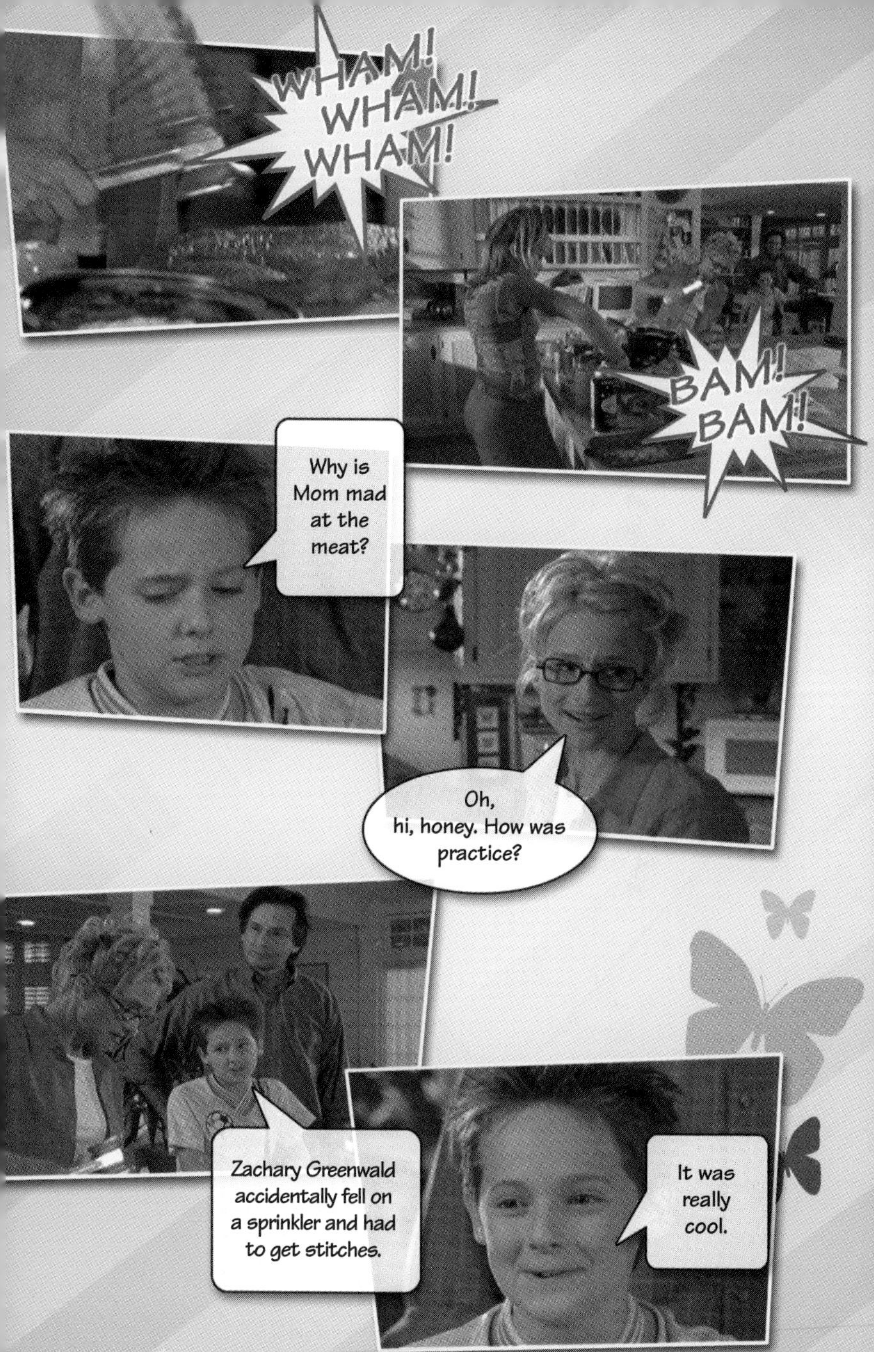
WHAM! WHAM! WHAM!
BAM! BAM!
Why is Mom mad at the meat?
Oh, hi, honey. How was practice?
Zachary Greenwald accidentally fell on a sprinkler and had to get stitches.
It was really cool.

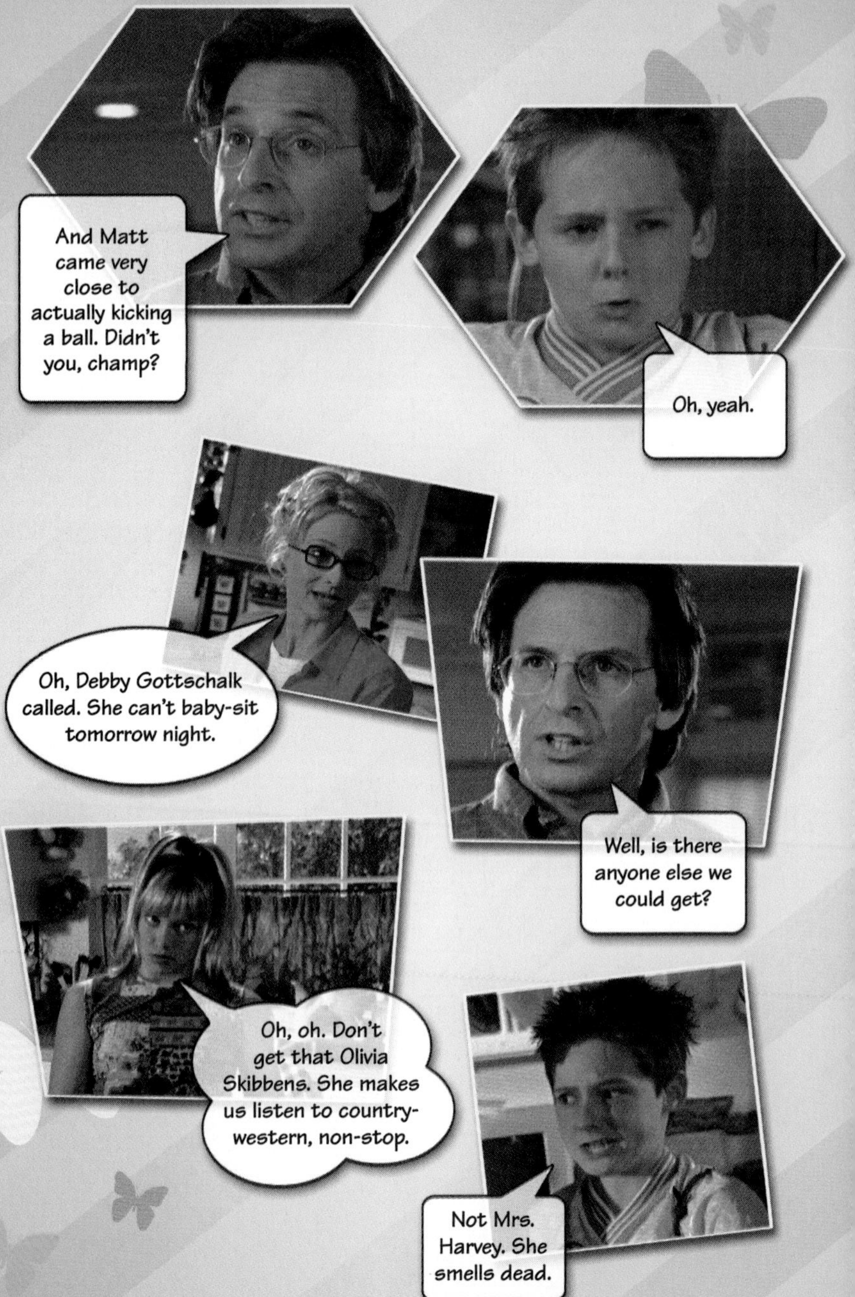
And Matt came very close to actually kicking a ball. Didn't you, champ?
Oh, yeah.
Oh, Debby Gottschalk called. She can't baby-sit tomorrow night.
Well, is there anyone else we could get?
Oh, oh. Don't get that Olivia Skibbens. She makes us listen to country-western, non-stop.
Not Mrs. Harvey. She smells dead.

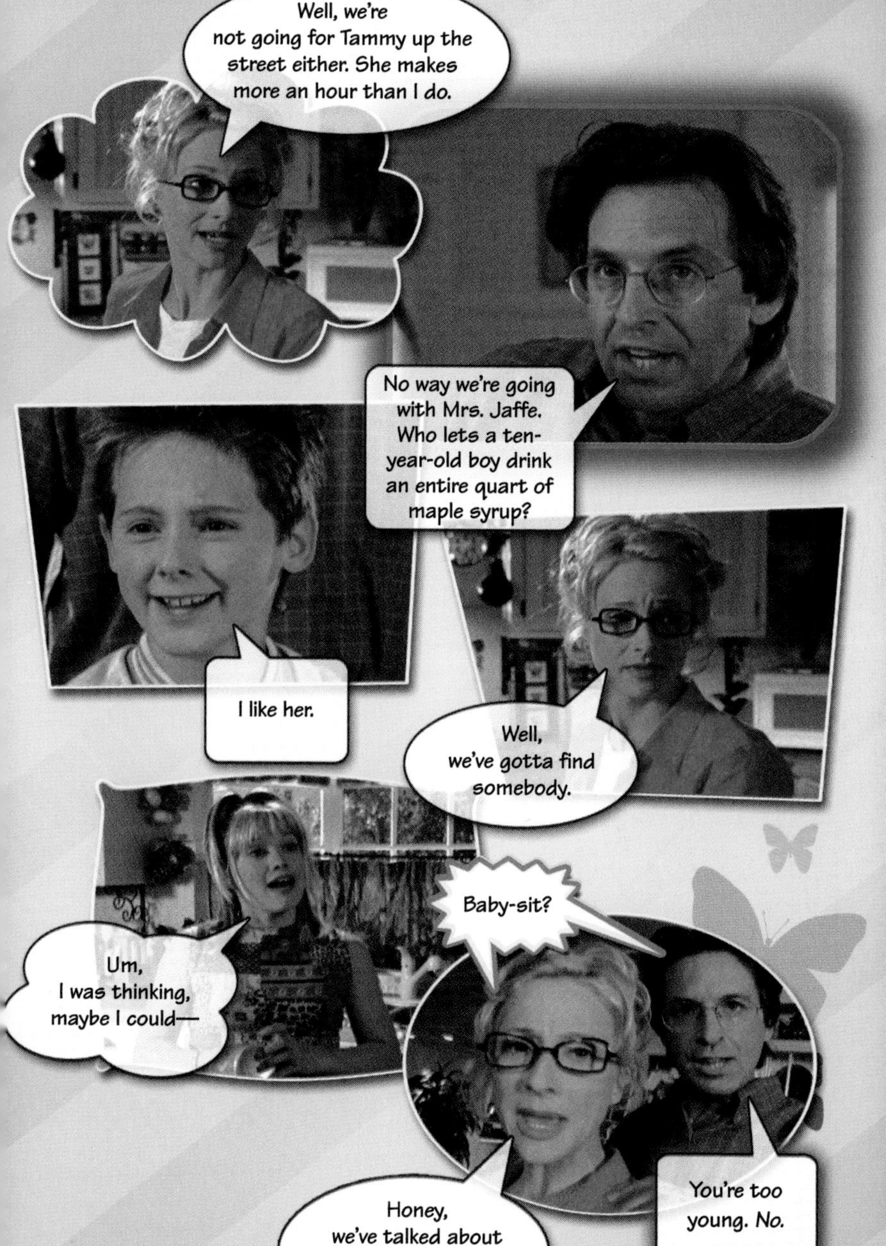
Well, we're not going for Tammy up the street either. She makes more an hour than I do.
No way we're going with Mrs. Jaffe. Who lets a ten-year-old boy drink an entire quart of maple syrup?
I like her.
Well, we've gotta find somebody.
Um, I was thinking, maybe I could—
Baby-sit?
Honey, we've talked about this, you know, we just think—
You're too young. No.

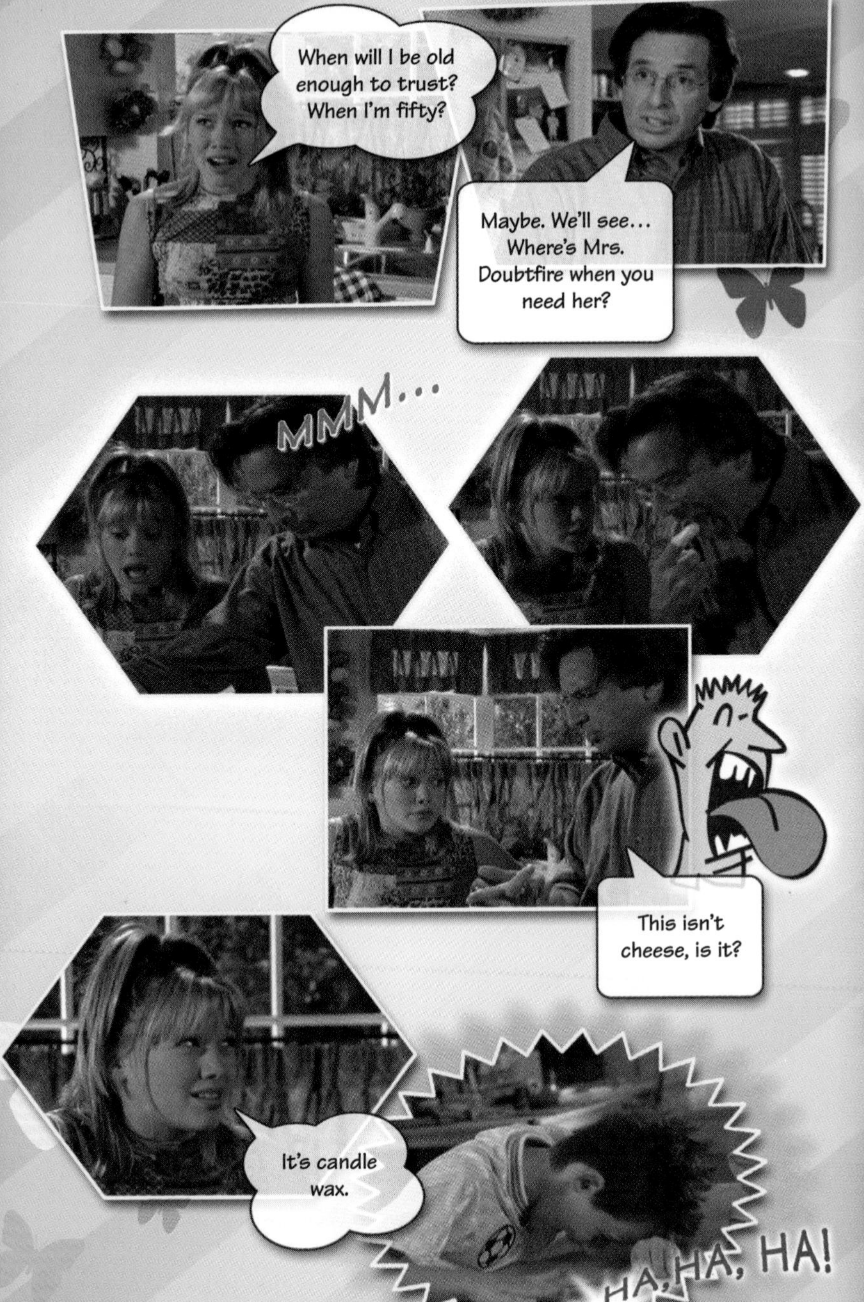
When will I be old enough to trust? When I'm fifty?
Maybe. We'll see… Where's Mrs. Doubtfire when you need her?
MMM…
This isn't cheese, is it?
It's candle wax.
HA, HA, HA!

AT SCHOOL...

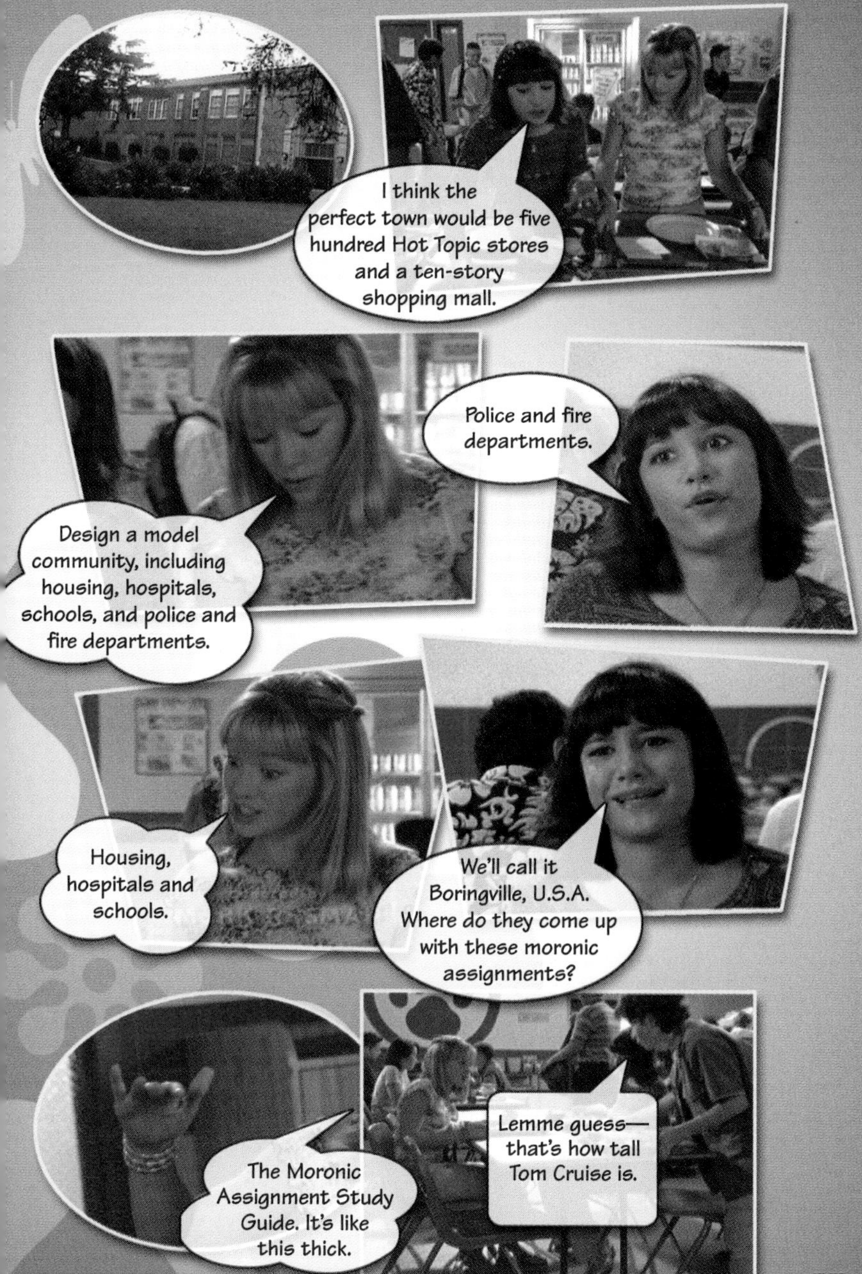
I think the perfect town would be five hundred Hot Topic stores and a ten-story shopping mall.
Design a model community, including housing, hospitals, schools, and police and fire departments.
Police and fire departments.
Housing, hospitals and schools.
We'll call it Boringville, U.S.A. Where do they come up with these moronic assignments?
The Moronic Assignment Study Guide. It's like this thick.
Lemme guess— that's how tall Tom Cruise is.

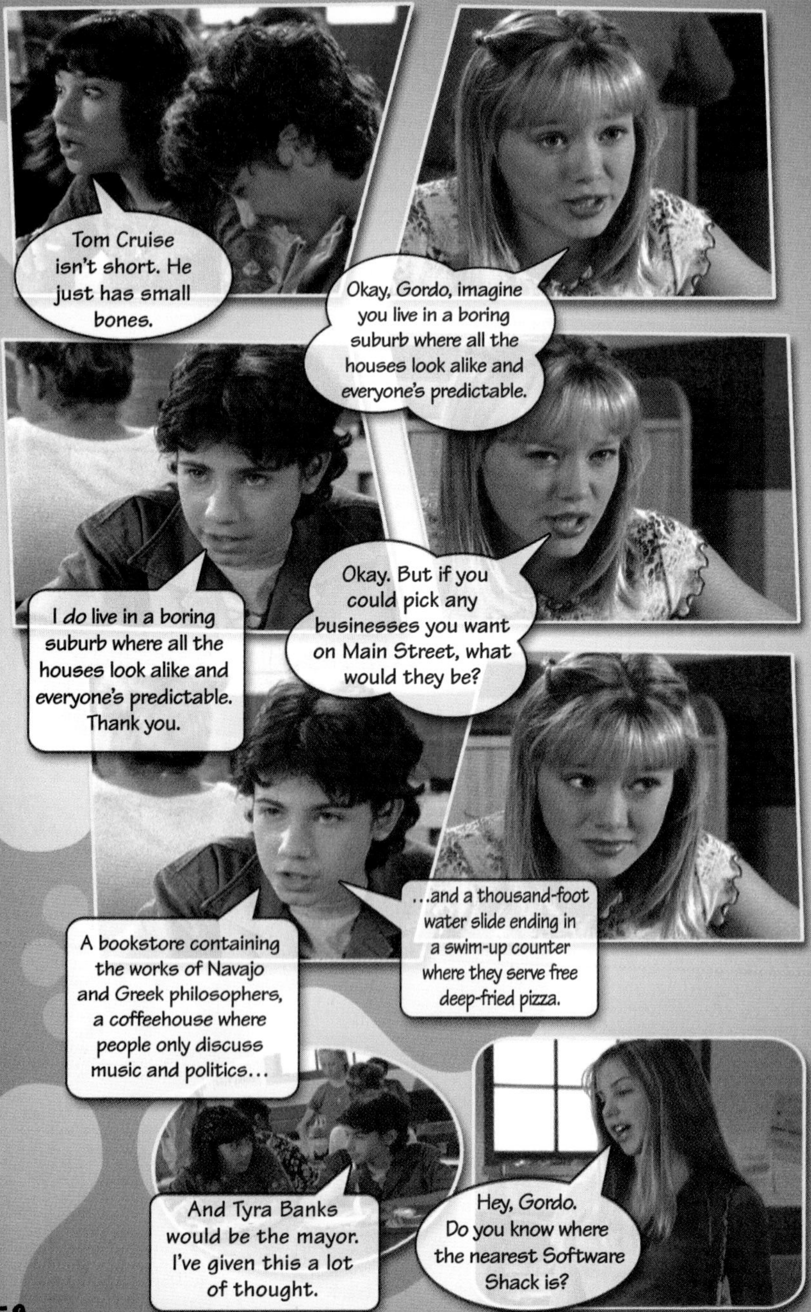
Tom Cruise isn't short. He just has small bones.
Okay, Gordo, imagine you live in a boring suburb where all the houses look alike and everyone's predictable.
I *do* live in a boring suburb where all the houses look alike and everyone's predictable. Thank you.
Okay. But if you could pick any businesses you want on Main Street, what would they be?
A bookstore containing the works of Navajo and Greek philosophers, a coffeehouse where people only discuss music and politics…
…and a thousand-foot water slide ending in a swim-up counter where they serve free deep-fried pizza.
And Tyra Banks would be the mayor. I've given this a lot of thought.
Hey, Gordo. Do you know where the nearest Software Shack is?

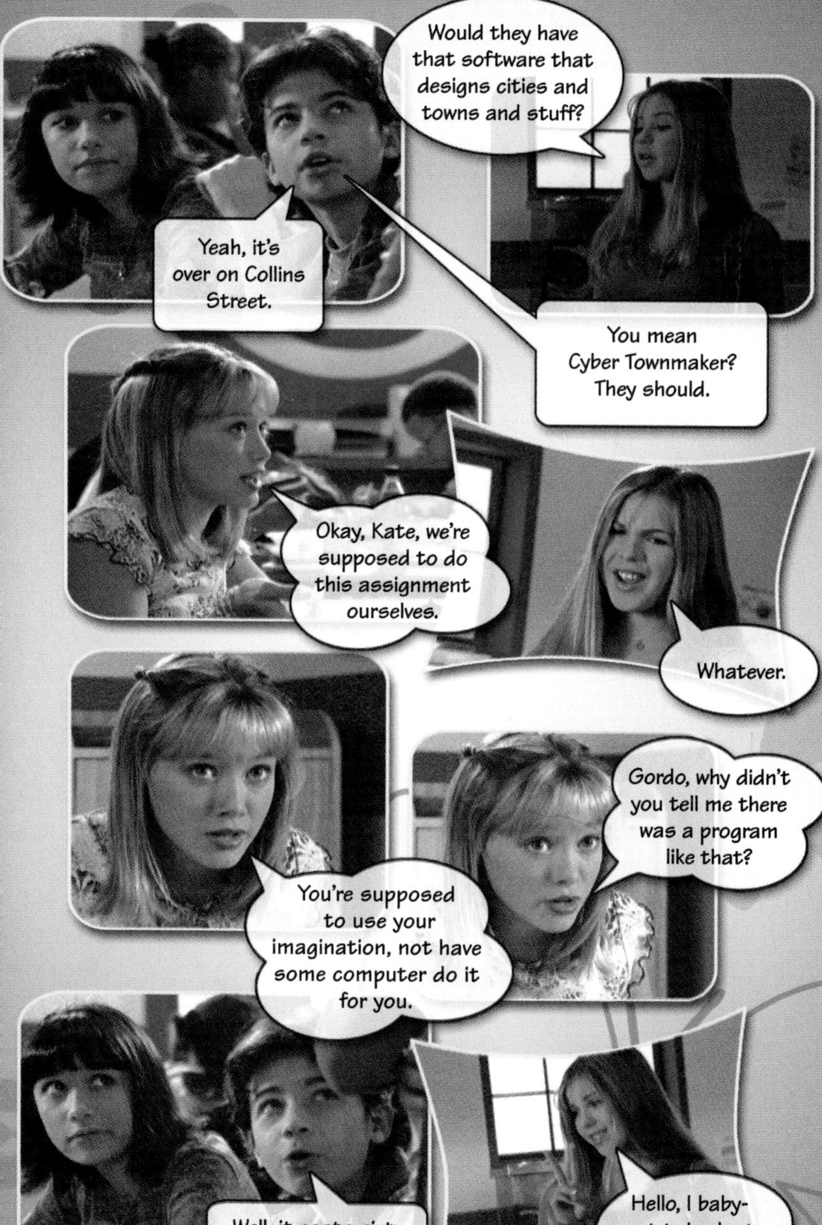
Yeah, it's over on Collins Street.
Would they have that software that designs cities and towns and stuff?
You mean Cyber Townmaker? They should.
Okay, Kate, we're supposed to do this assignment ourselves.
Whatever.
You're supposed to use your imagination, not have some computer do it for you.
Gordo, why didn't you tell me there was a program like that?
Well, it costs sixty bucks. I don't think you can afford it.
Hello, I baby-sat twice last week.

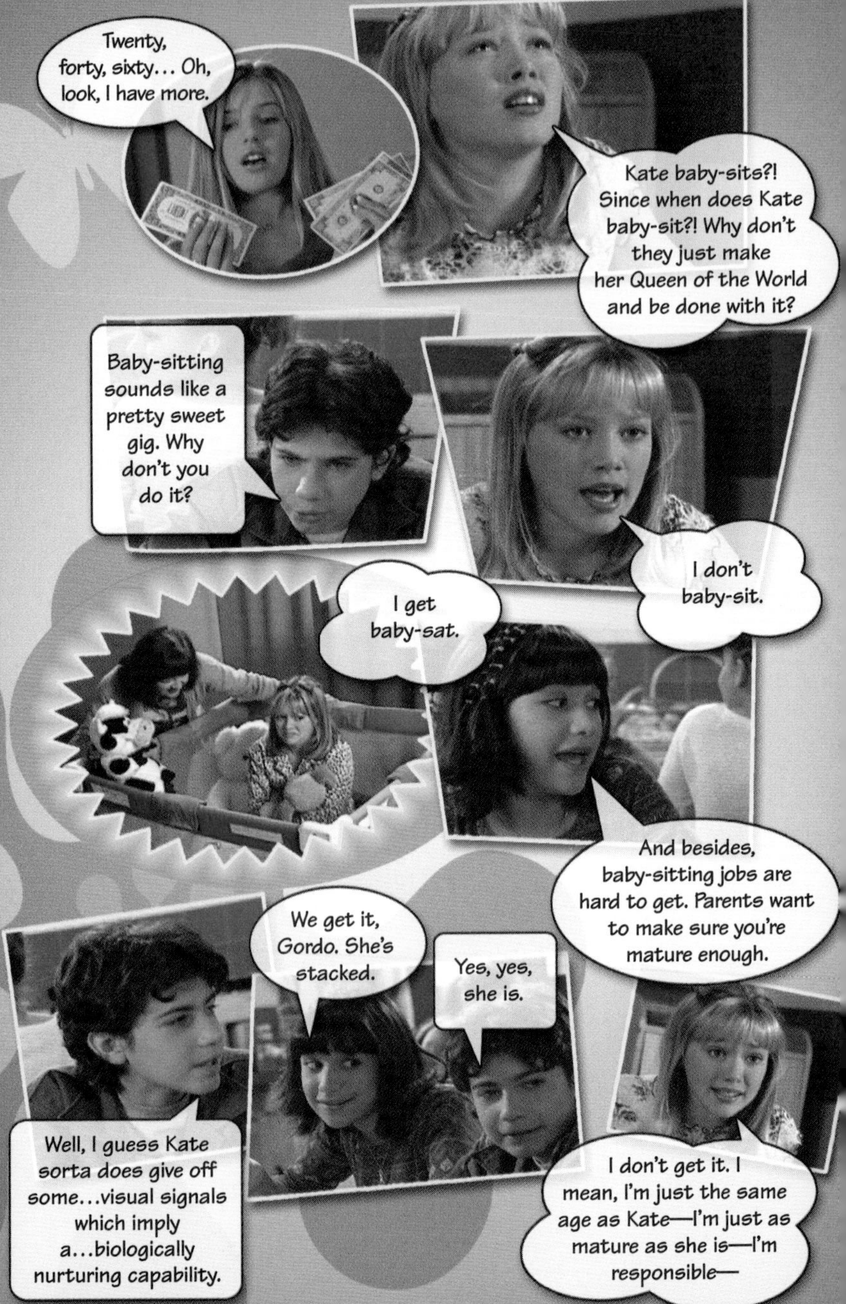
Twenty, forty, sixty… Oh, look, I have more.
Kate baby-sits?! Since when does Kate baby-sit?! Why don't they just make her Queen of the World and be done with it?
Baby-sitting sounds like a pretty sweet gig. Why don't you do it?
I don't baby-sit.
I get baby-sat.
And besides, baby-sitting jobs are hard to get. Parents want to make sure you're mature enough.
Well, I guess Kate sorta does give off some…visual signals which imply a…biologically nurturing capability.
We get it, Gordo. She's stacked.
Yes, yes, she is.
I don't get it. I mean, I'm just the same age as Kate—I'm just as mature as she is—I'm responsible—

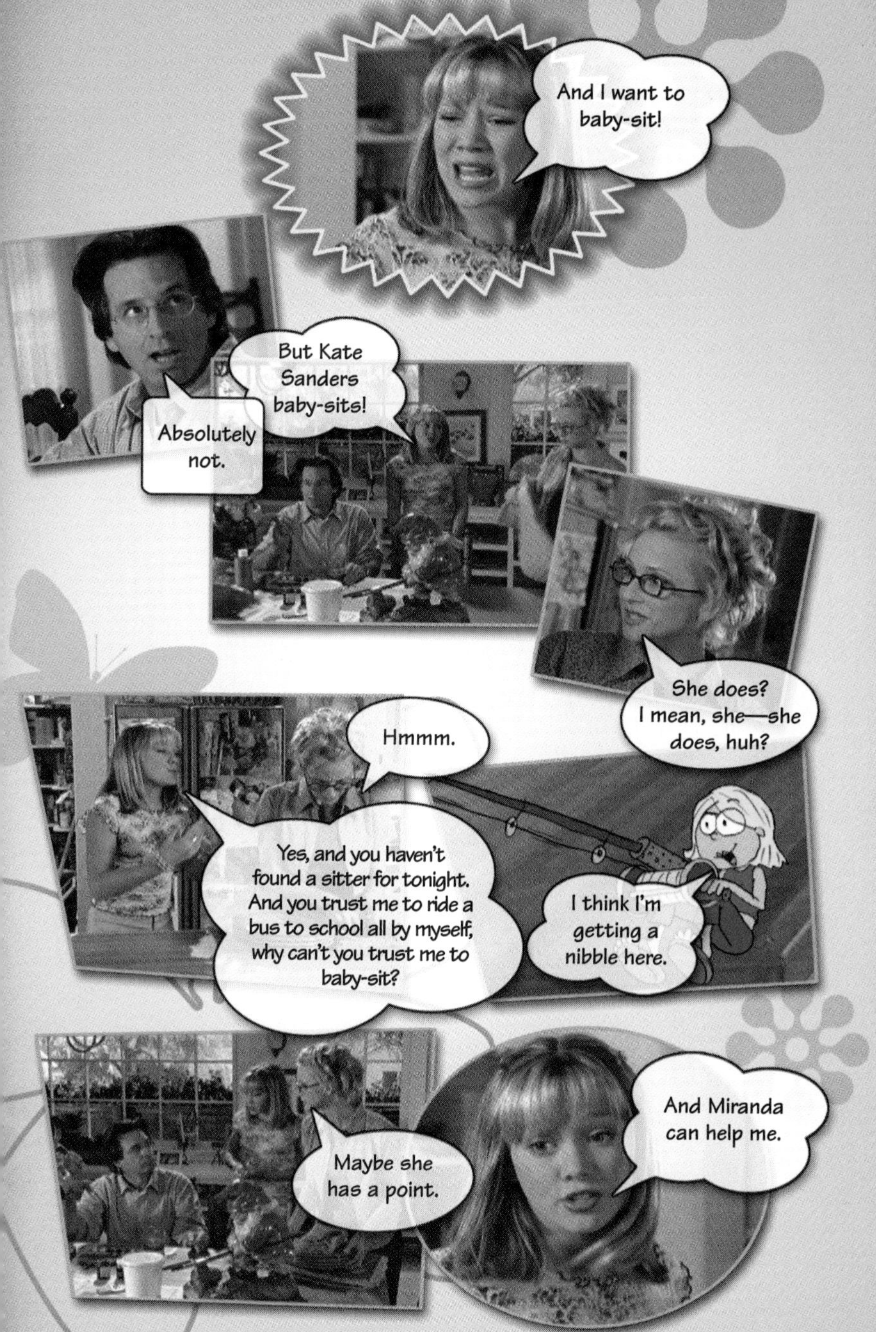
And I want to baby-sit!
Absolutely not.
But Kate Sanders baby-sits!
She does? I mean, she—she does, huh?
Hmmm.
Yes, and you haven't found a sitter for tonight. And you trust me to ride a bus to school all by myself, why can't you trust me to baby-sit?
I think I'm getting a nibble here.
Maybe she has a point.
And Miranda can help me.

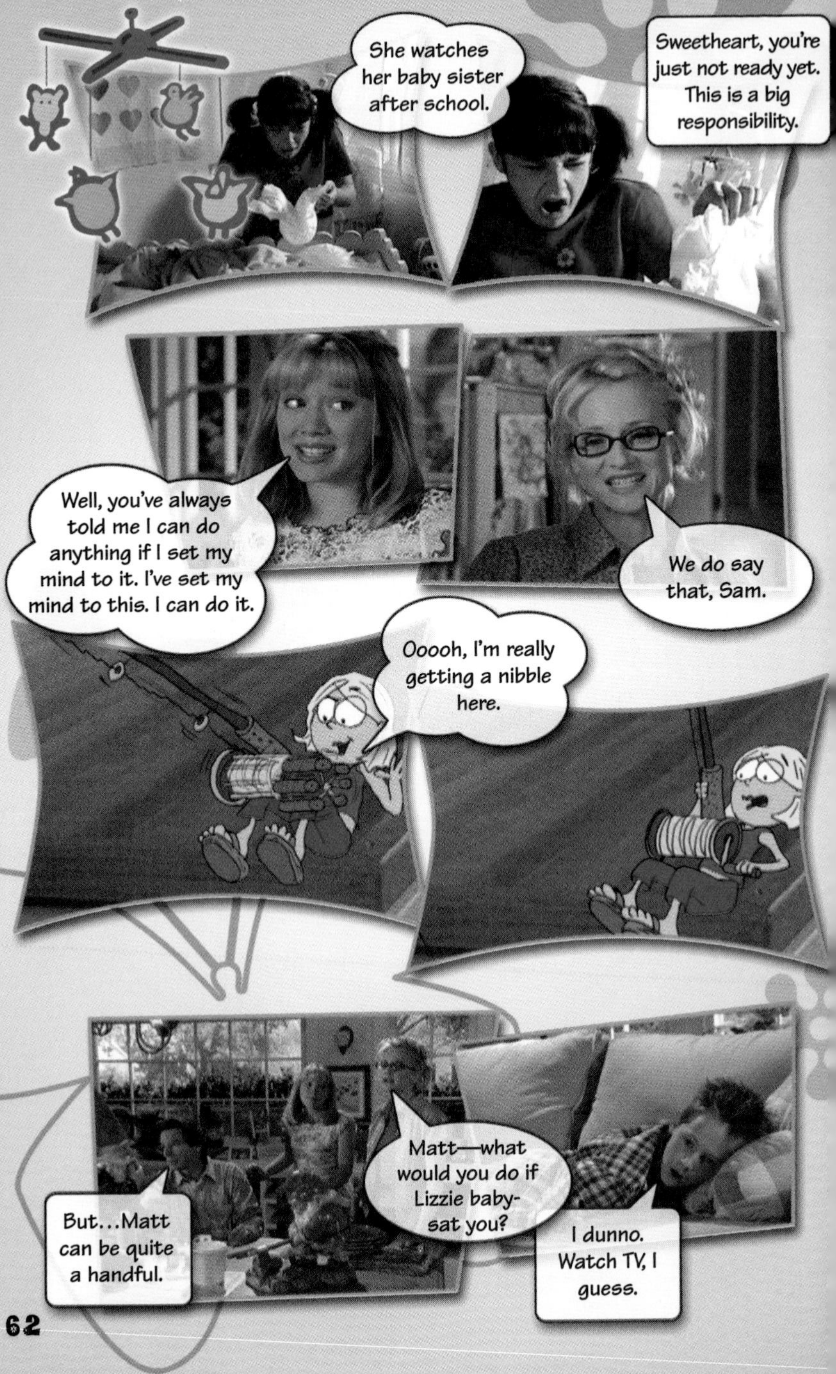
She watches her baby sister after school.
Sweetheart, you're just not ready yet. This is a big responsibility.
Well, you've always told me I can do anything if I set my mind to it. I've set my mind to this. I can do it.
We do say that, Sam.
Ooooh, I'm really getting a nibble here.
But...Matt can be quite a handful.
Matt—what would you do if Lizzie baby-sat you?
I dunno. Watch TV, I guess.

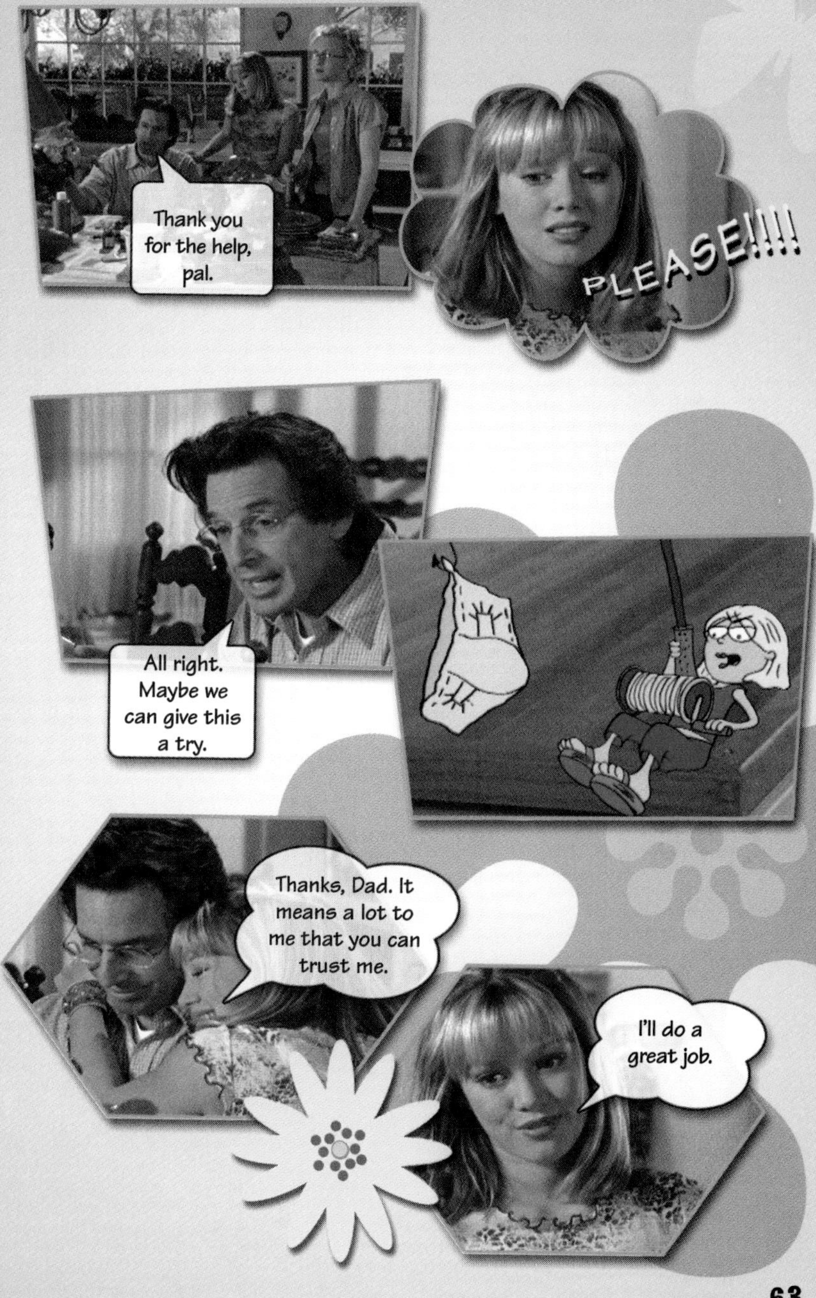
Thank you for the help, pal.
PLEASE!!!!
All right. Maybe we can give this a try.
Thanks, Dad. It means a lot to me that you can trust me.
I'll do a great job.

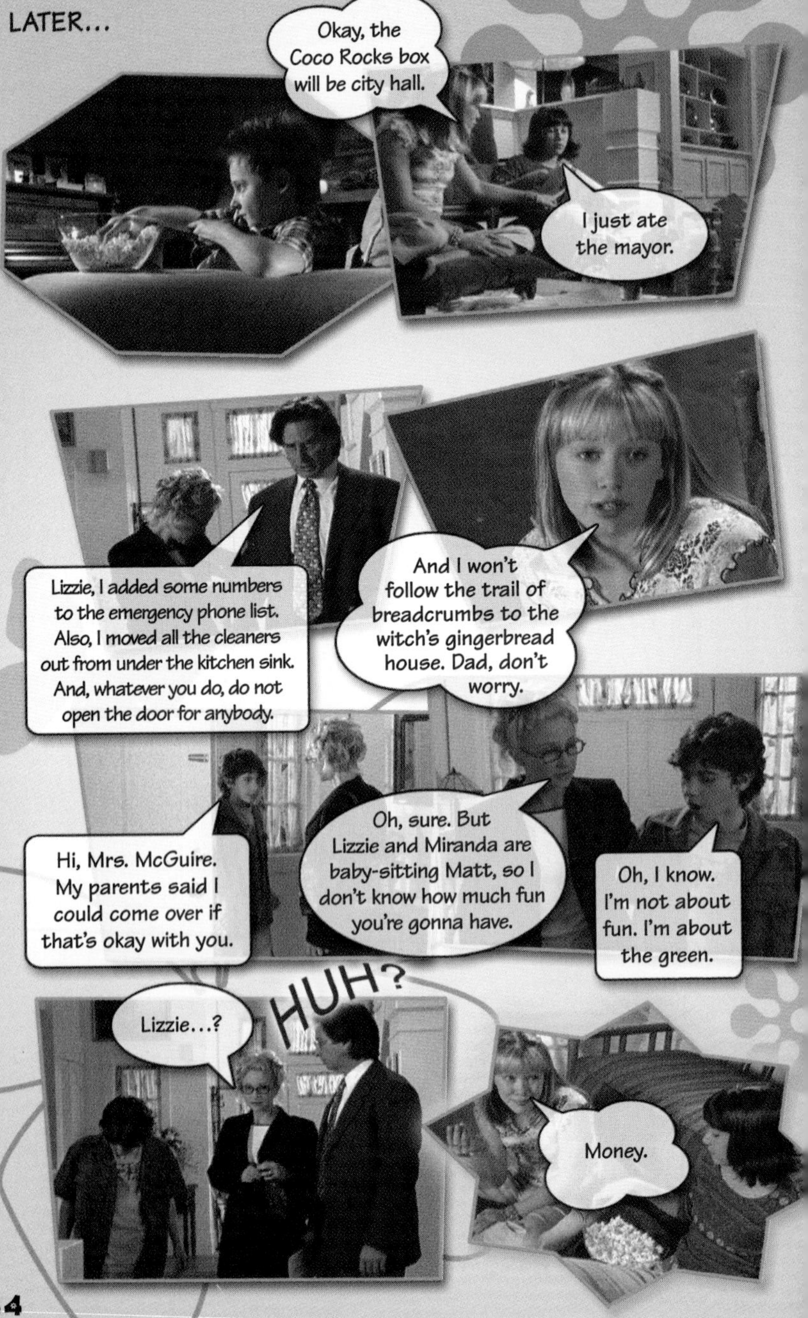
LATER...
Okay, the Coco Rocks box will be city hall.
I just ate the mayor.
Lizzie, I added some numbers to the emergency phone list. Also, I moved all the cleaners out from under the kitchen sink. And, whatever you do, do not open the door for anybody.
And I won't follow the trail of breadcrumbs to the witch's gingerbread house. Dad, don't worry.
Hi, Mrs. McGuire. My parents said I could come over if that's okay with you.
Oh, sure. But Lizzie and Miranda are baby-sitting Matt, so I don't know how much fun you're gonna have.
Oh, I know. I'm not about fun. I'm about the green.
Lizzie...?
HUH?
Money.

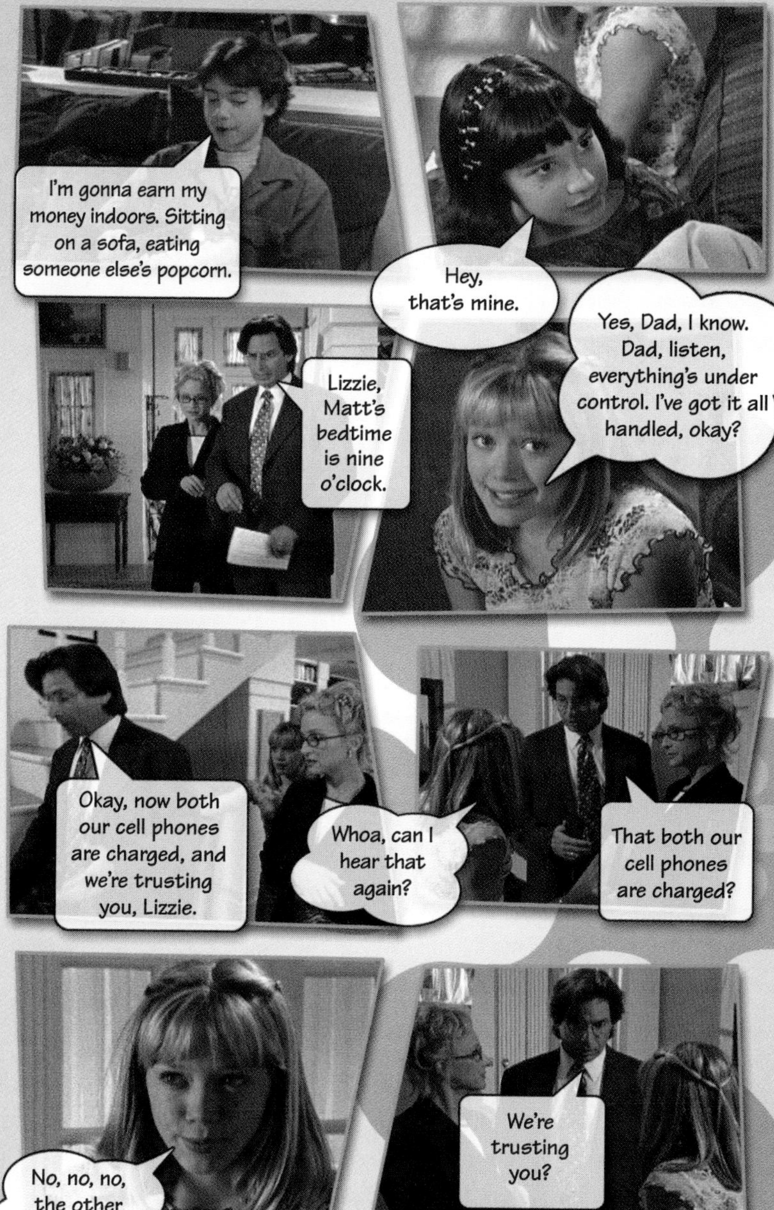
I'm gonna earn my money indoors. Sitting on a sofa, eating someone else's popcorn.
Hey, that's mine.
Lizzie, Matt's bedtime is nine o'clock.
Yes, Dad, I know. Dad, listen, everything's under control. I've got it all handled, okay?
Okay, now both our cell phones are charged, and we're trusting you, Lizzie.
Whoa, can I hear that again?
That both our cell phones are charged?
No, no, no, the other part.
We're trusting you?

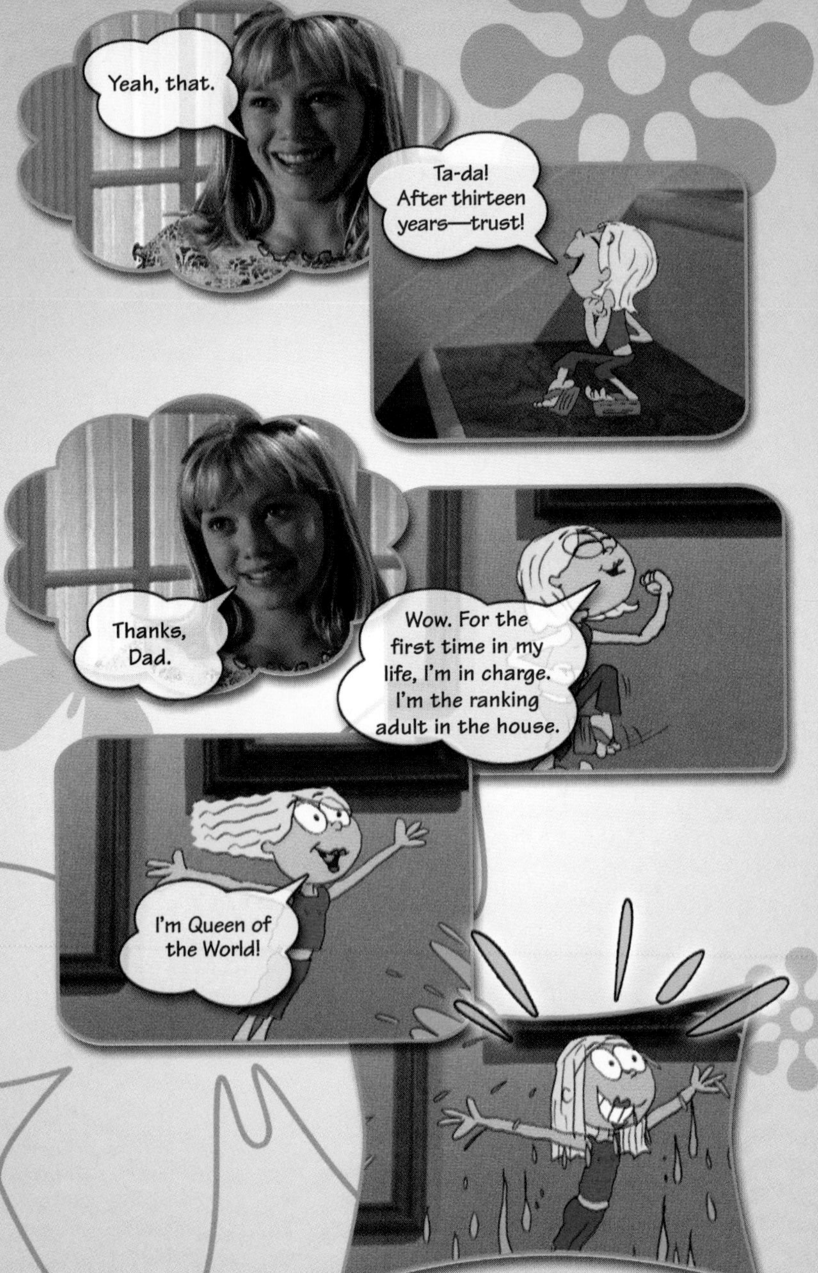
Yeah, that.
Ta-da! After thirteen years—trust!
Thanks, Dad.
Wow. For the first time in my life, I'm in charge. I'm the ranking adult in the house.
I'm Queen of the World!

Alone at last.
I don't see why you have to muscle in on baby-sitting, Gordo. This is how we make money.
Why should girls have a monopoly on baby-sitting?
Because boys have a monopoly on burping the Pledge of Allegiance. We deserve some kind of monopoly.
Hey, I love that game. I wanna be the racecar!
Tough luck. You're gonna watch Willie Wonka.
I've seen that ten times. I wanna be the racecar!
Well, we've got homework. If you'll be patient, we'll maybe play later. Okay?
All right.

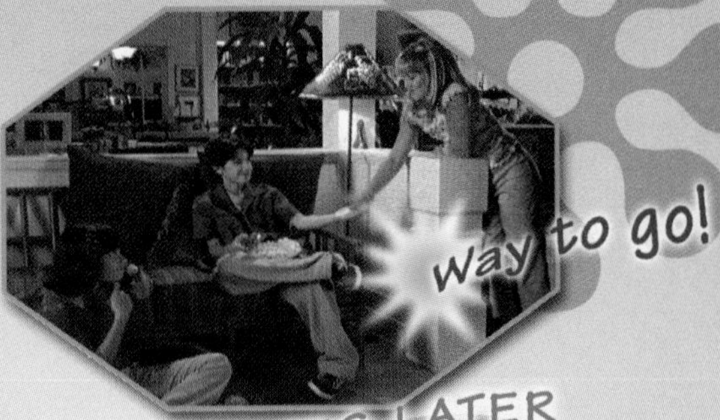
way to go!

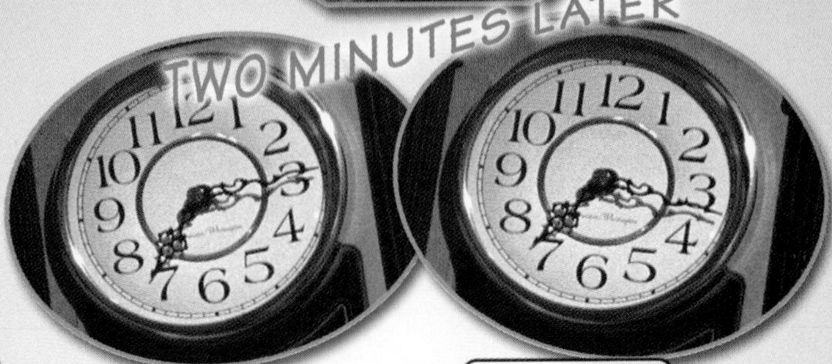
TWO MINUTES LATER

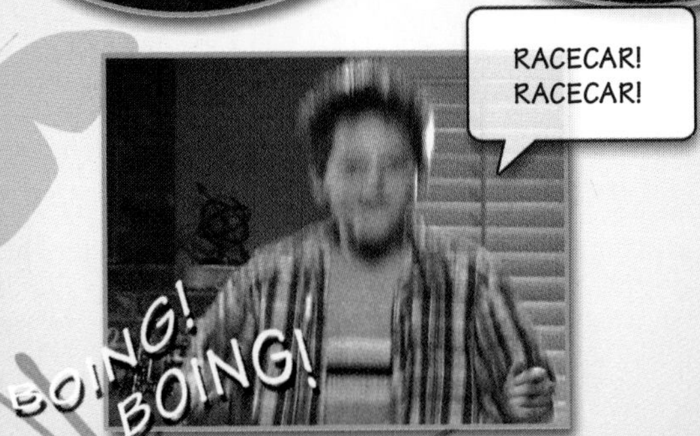
RACECAR!
RACECAR!
BOING!
BOING!

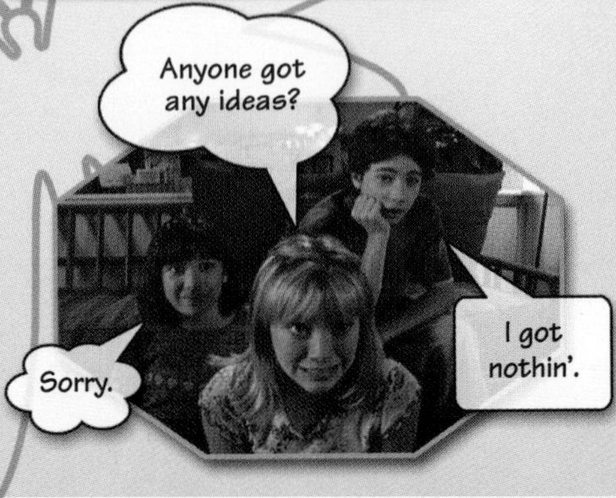
Anyone got any ideas?
Sorry.
I got nothin'.

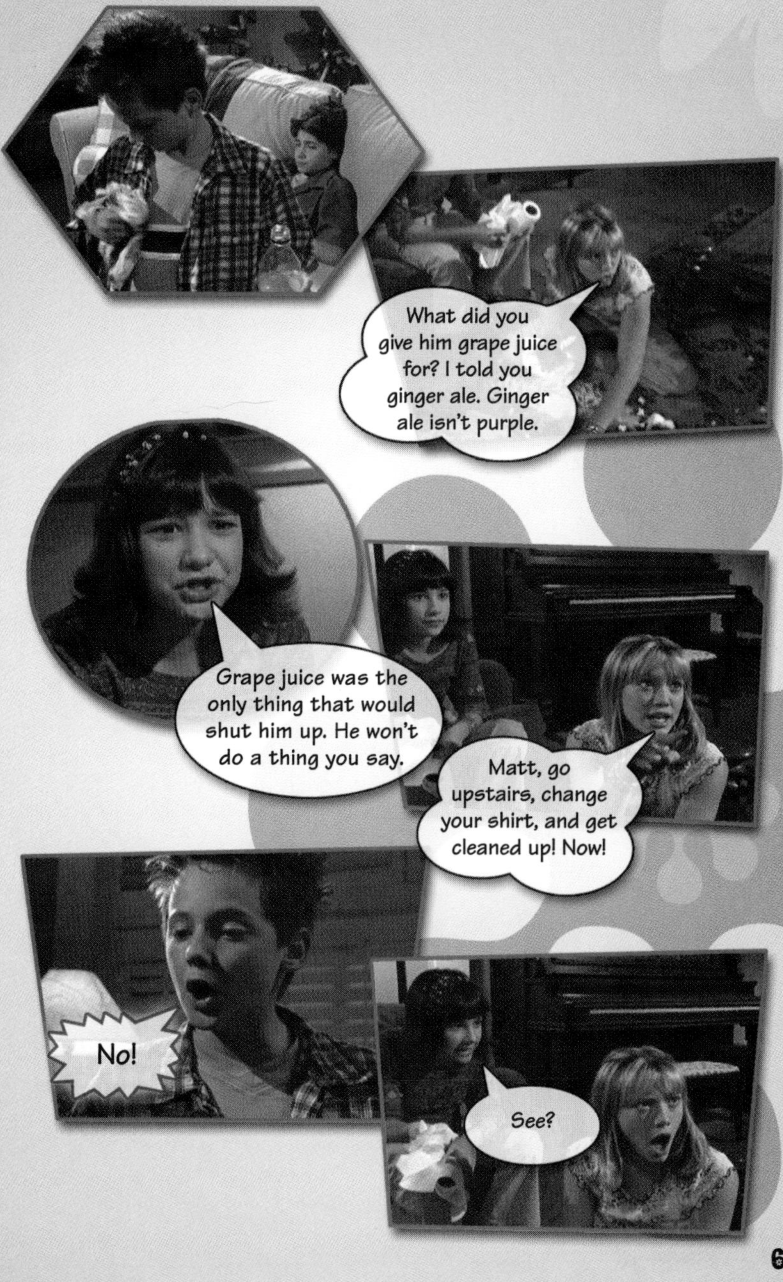
What did you give him grape juice for? I told you ginger ale. Ginger ale isn't purple.
Grape juice was the only thing that would shut him up. He won't do a thing you say.
Matt, go upstairs, change your shirt, and get cleaned up! Now!
No!
See?

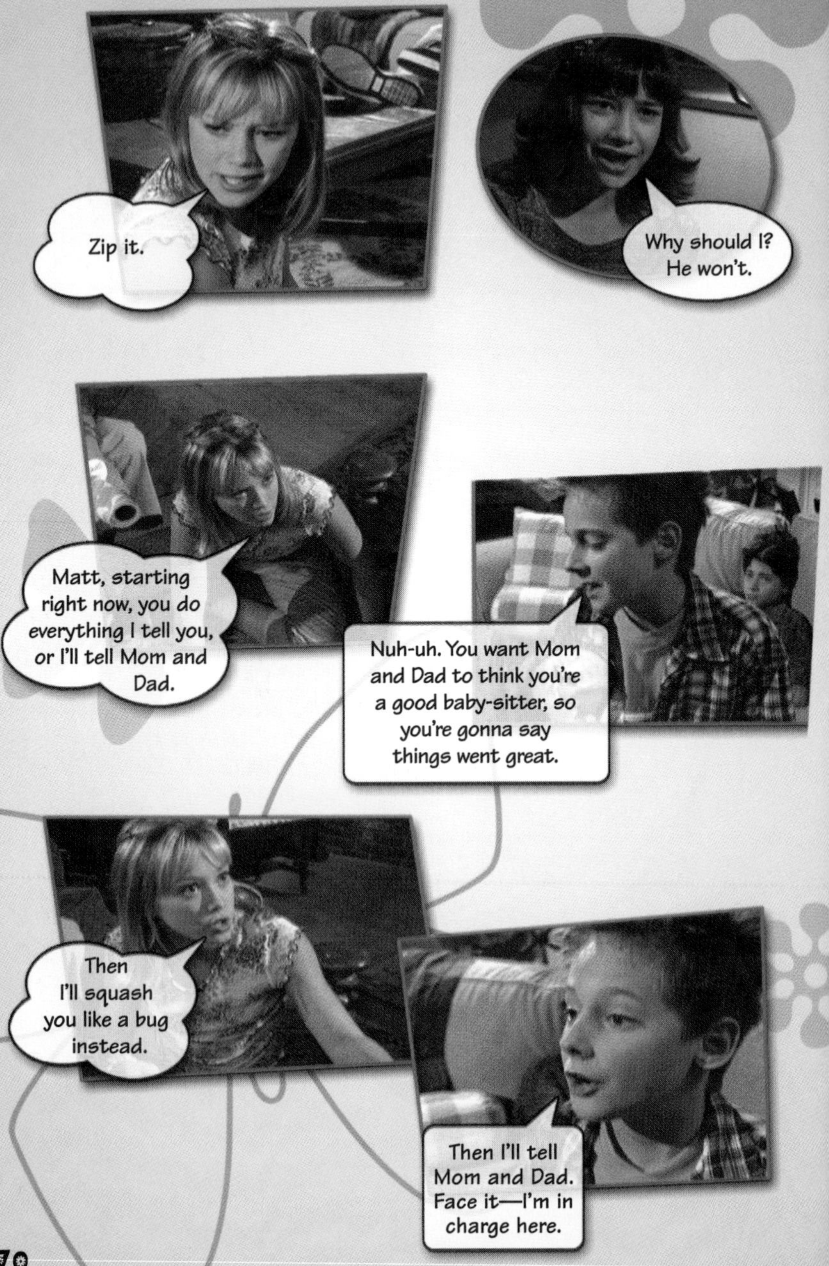
Zip it.
Why should I? He won't.
Matt, starting right now, you do everything I tell you, or I'll tell Mom and Dad.
Nuh-uh. You want Mom and Dad to think you're a good baby-sitter, so you're gonna say things went great.
Then I'll squash you like a bug instead.
Then I'll tell Mom and Dad. Face it—I'm in charge here.

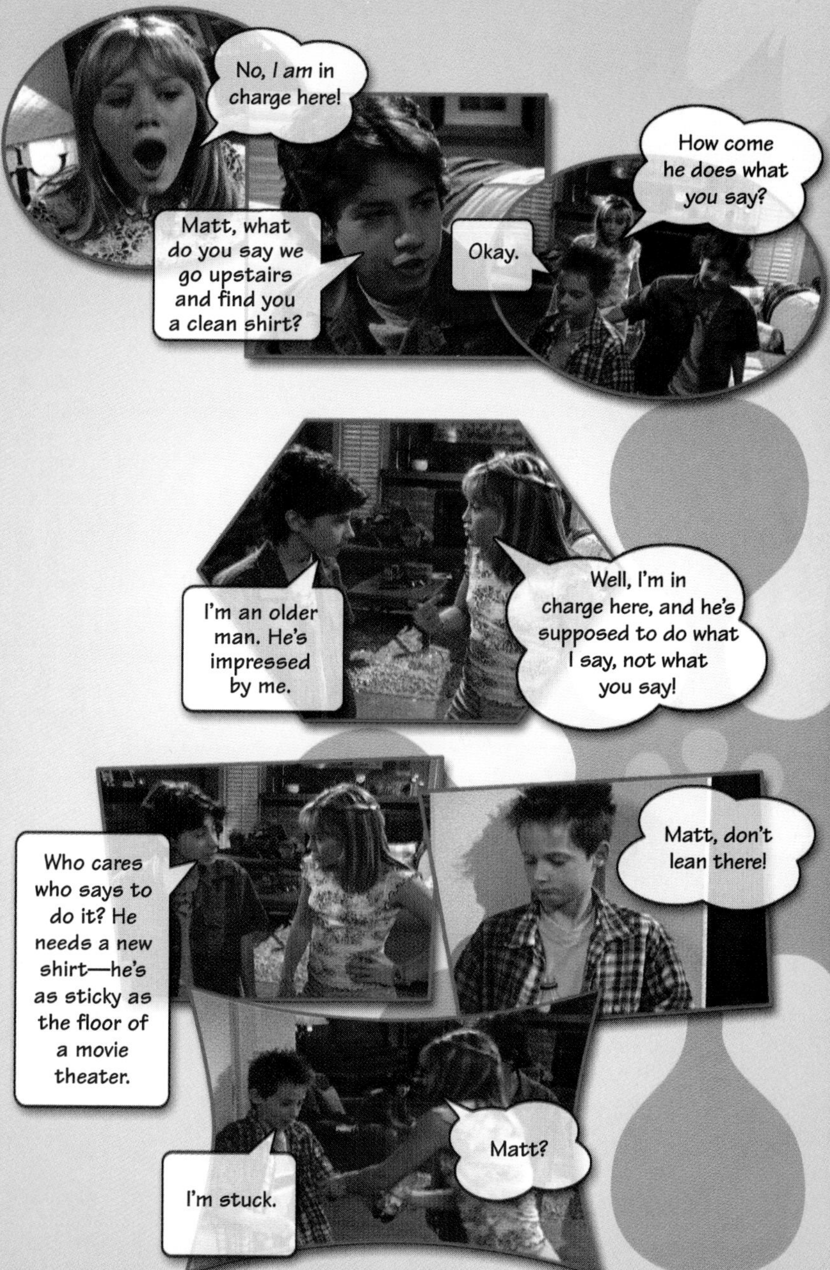

No, *I am* in charge here!
Matt, what do you say we go upstairs and find you a clean shirt?
Okay.
How come he does what you say?
I'm an older man. He's impressed by me.
Well, I'm in charge here, and he's supposed to do what I say, not what you say!
Who cares who says to do it? He needs a new shirt—he's as sticky as the floor of a movie theater.
Matt, don't lean there!
Matt?
I'm stuck.

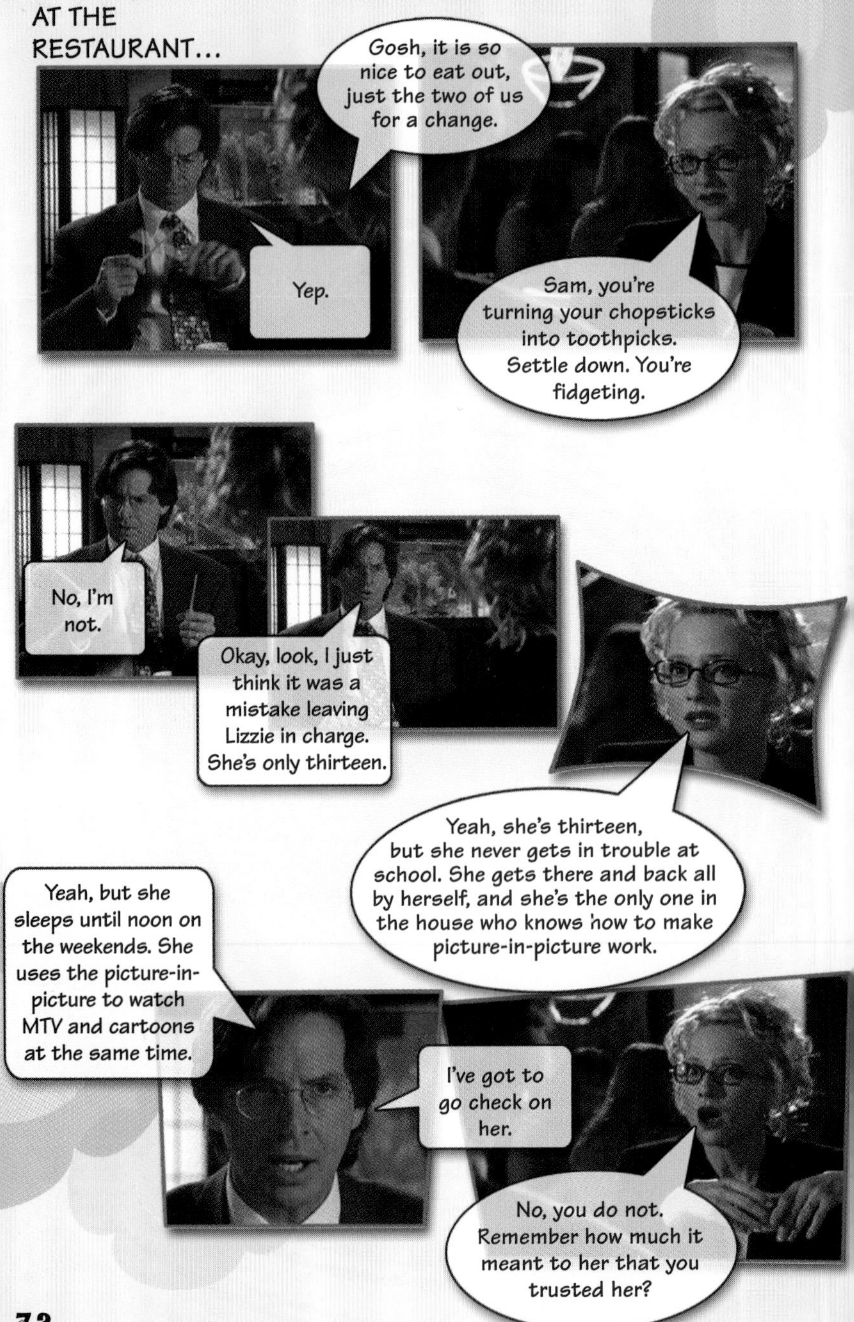
AT THE RESTAURANT...
Gosh, it is so nice to eat out, just the two of us for a change.
Yep.
Sam, you're turning your chopsticks into toothpicks. Settle down. You're fidgeting.
No, I'm not.
Okay, look, I just think it was a mistake leaving Lizzie in charge. She's only thirteen.
Yeah, she's thirteen, but she never gets in trouble at school. She gets there and back all by herself, and she's the only one in the house who knows how to make picture-in-picture work.
Yeah, but she sleeps until noon on the weekends. She uses the picture-in-picture to watch MTV and cartoons at the same time.
I've got to go check on her.
No, you do not. Remember how much it meant to her that you trusted her?

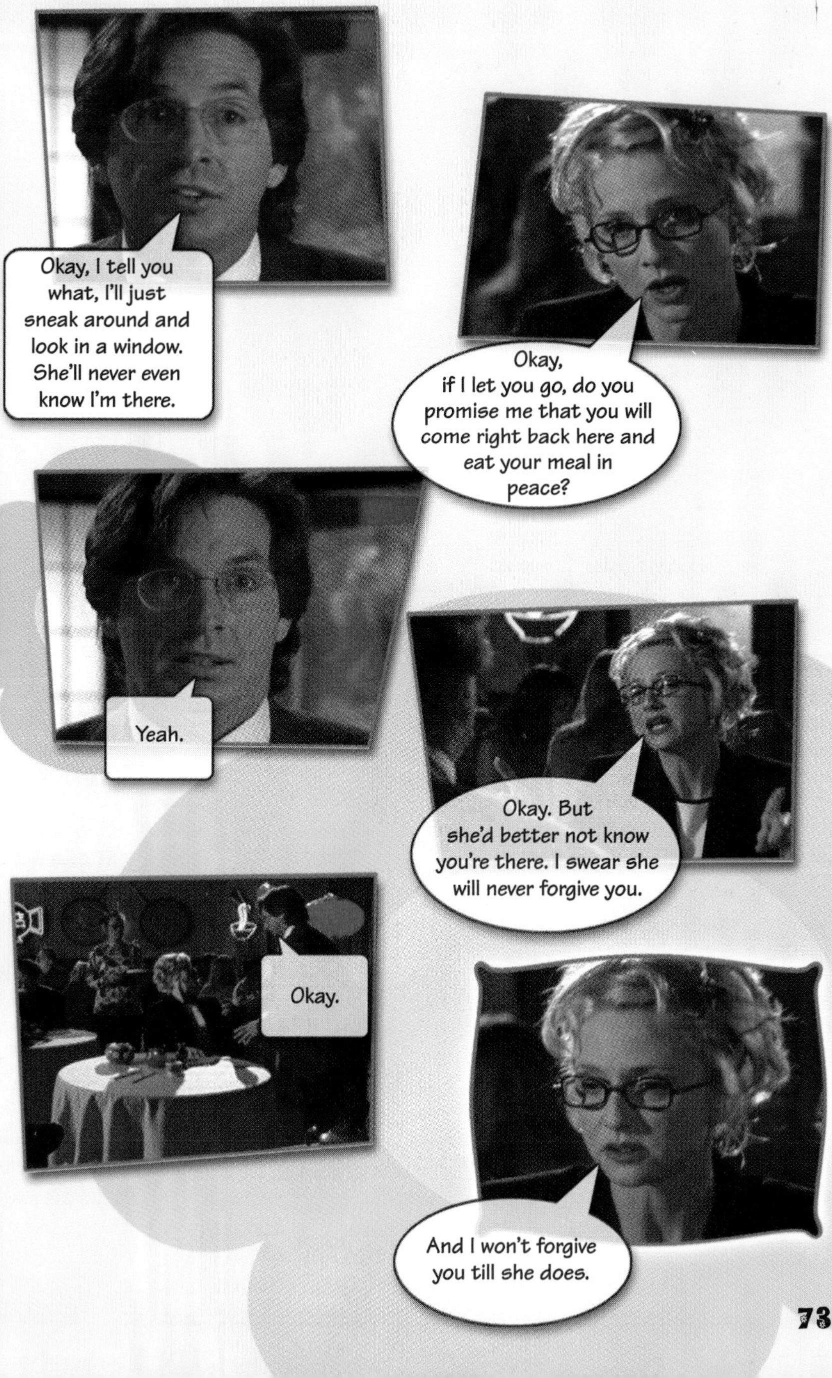
Okay, I tell you what, I'll just sneak around and look in a window. She'll never even know I'm there.
Okay, if I let you go, do you promise me that you will come right back here and eat your meal in peace?
Yeah.
Okay. But she'd better not know you're there. I swear she will never forgive you.
Okay.
And I won't forgive you till she does.

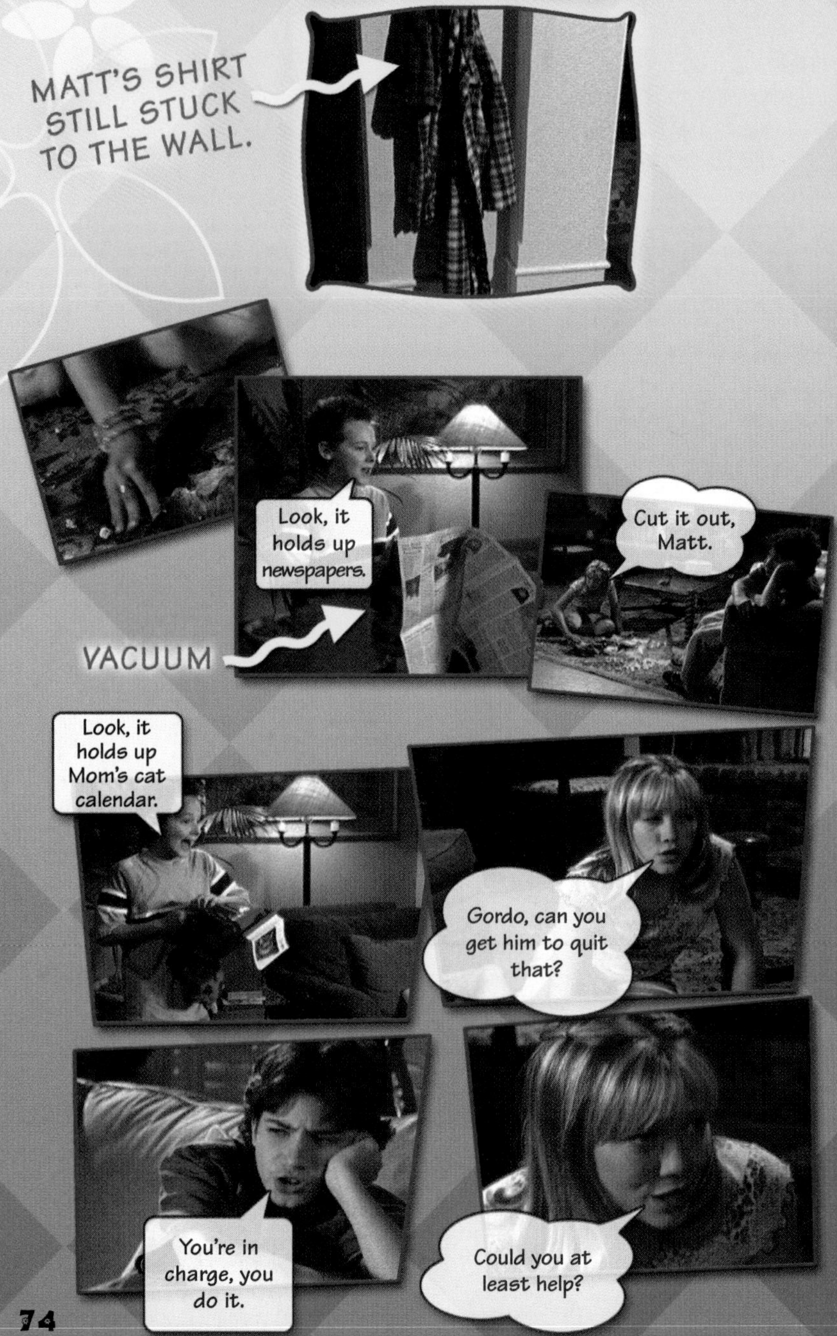
MATT'S SHIRT STILL STUCK TO THE WALL.
Look, it holds up newspapers.
VACUUM
Cut it out, Matt.
Look, it holds up Mom's cat calendar.
Gordo, can you get him to quit that?
You're in charge, you do it.
Could you at least help?

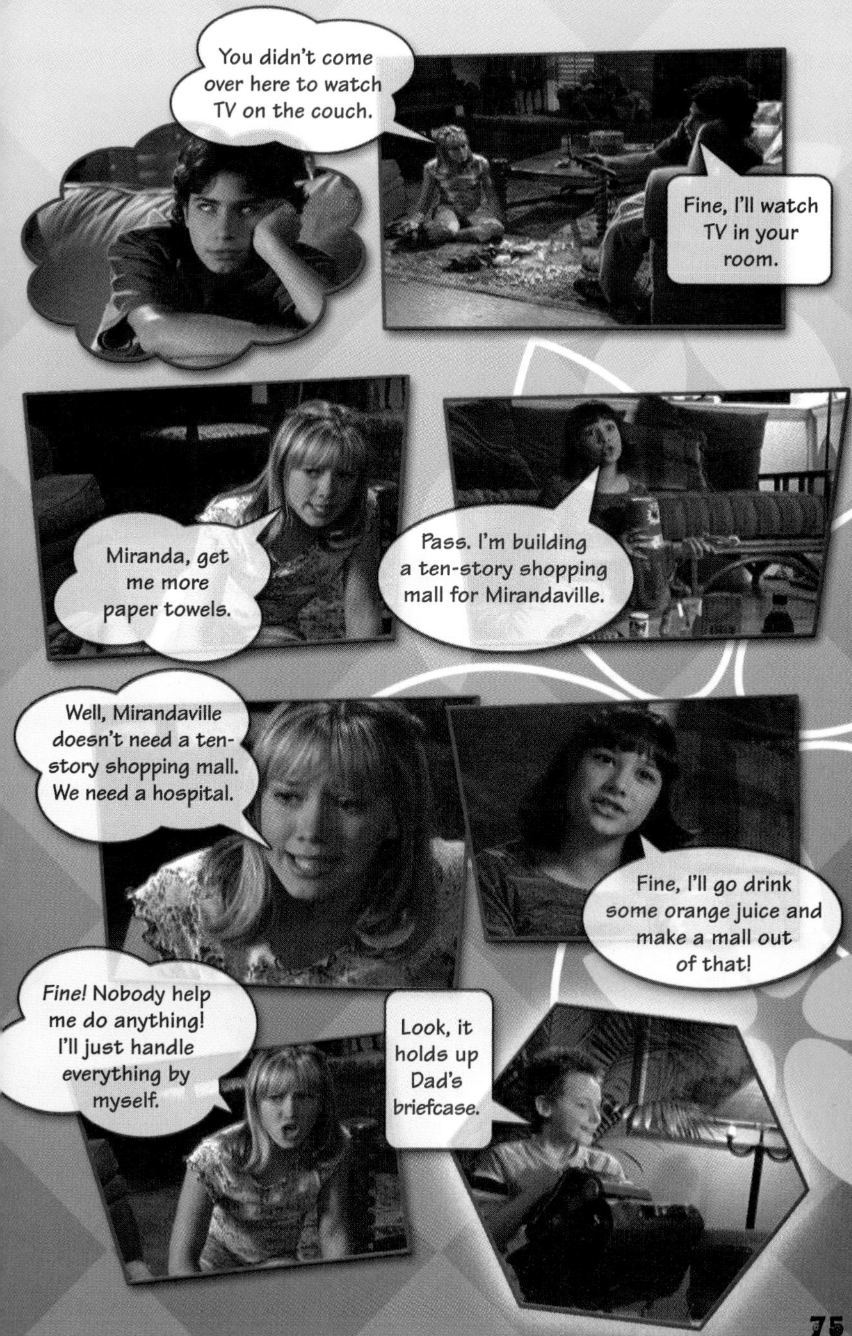

You didn't come over here to watch TV on the couch.
Fine, I'll watch TV in your room.
Miranda, get me more paper towels.
Pass. I'm building a ten-story shopping mall for Mirandaville.
Well, Mirandaville doesn't need a ten-story shopping mall. We need a hospital.
Fine, I'll go drink some orange juice and make a mall out of that!
Fine! Nobody help me do anything! I'll just handle everything by myself.
Look, it holds up Dad's briefcase.

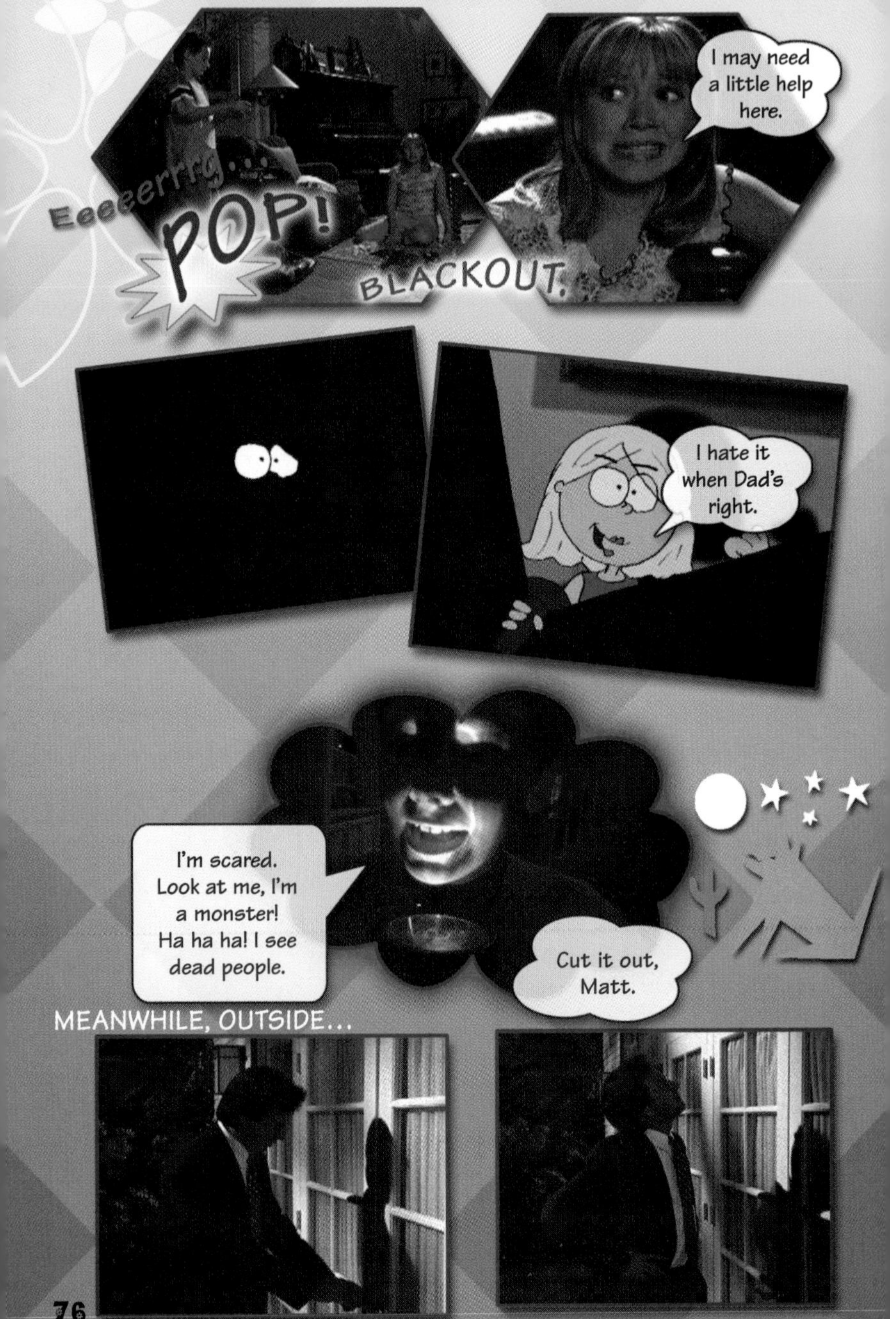

Eeeeerrrg...
POP!
BLACKOUT.
I may need a little help here.
I hate it when Dad's right.
I'm scared. Look at me, I'm a monster! Ha ha ha! I see dead people.
Cut it out, Matt.
MEANWHILE, OUTSIDE...

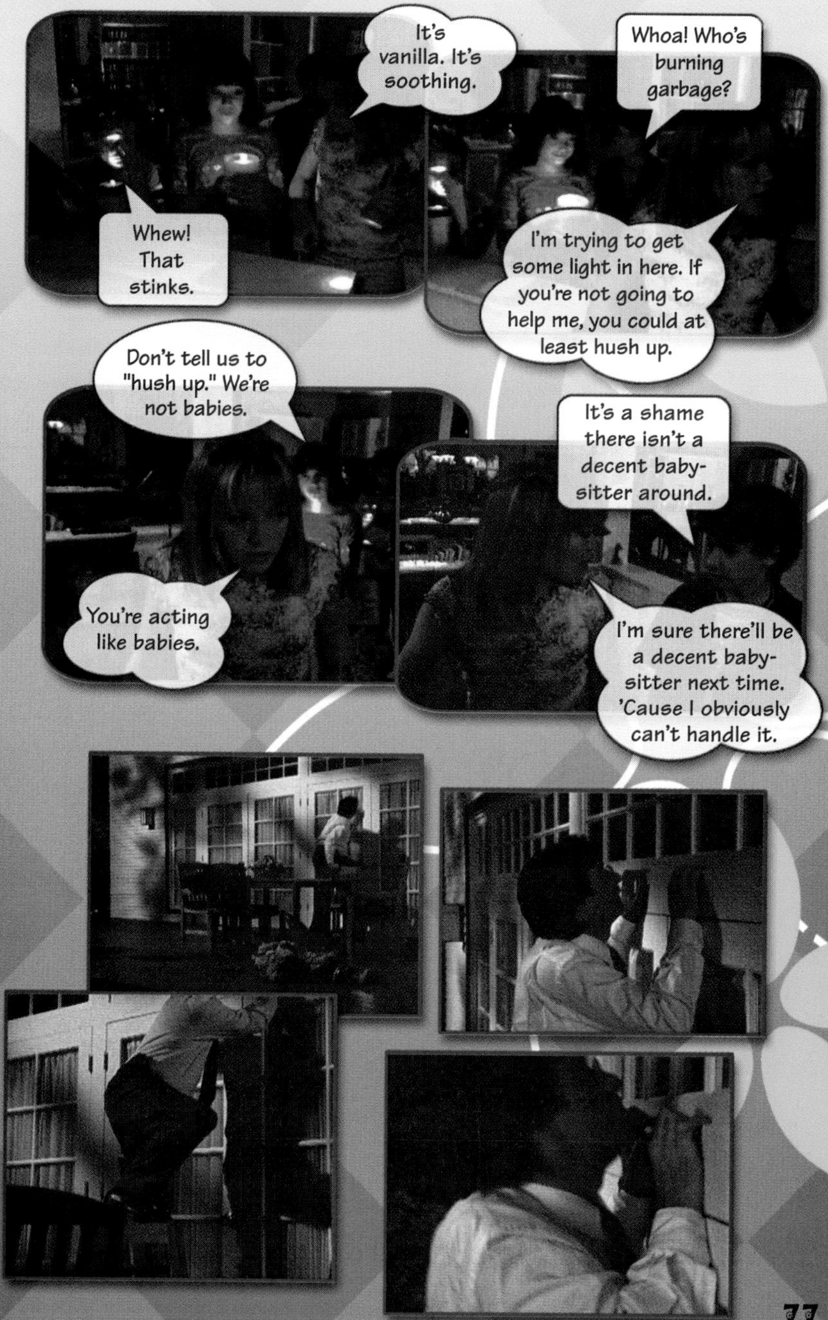
Whew! That stinks.
It's vanilla. It's soothing.
Whoa! Who's burning garbage?
I'm trying to get some light in here. If you're not going to help me, you could at least hush up.
Don't tell us to "hush up." We're not babies.
You're acting like babies.
It's a shame there isn't a decent baby-sitter around.
I'm sure there'll be a decent baby-sitter next time. 'Cause I obviously can't handle it.

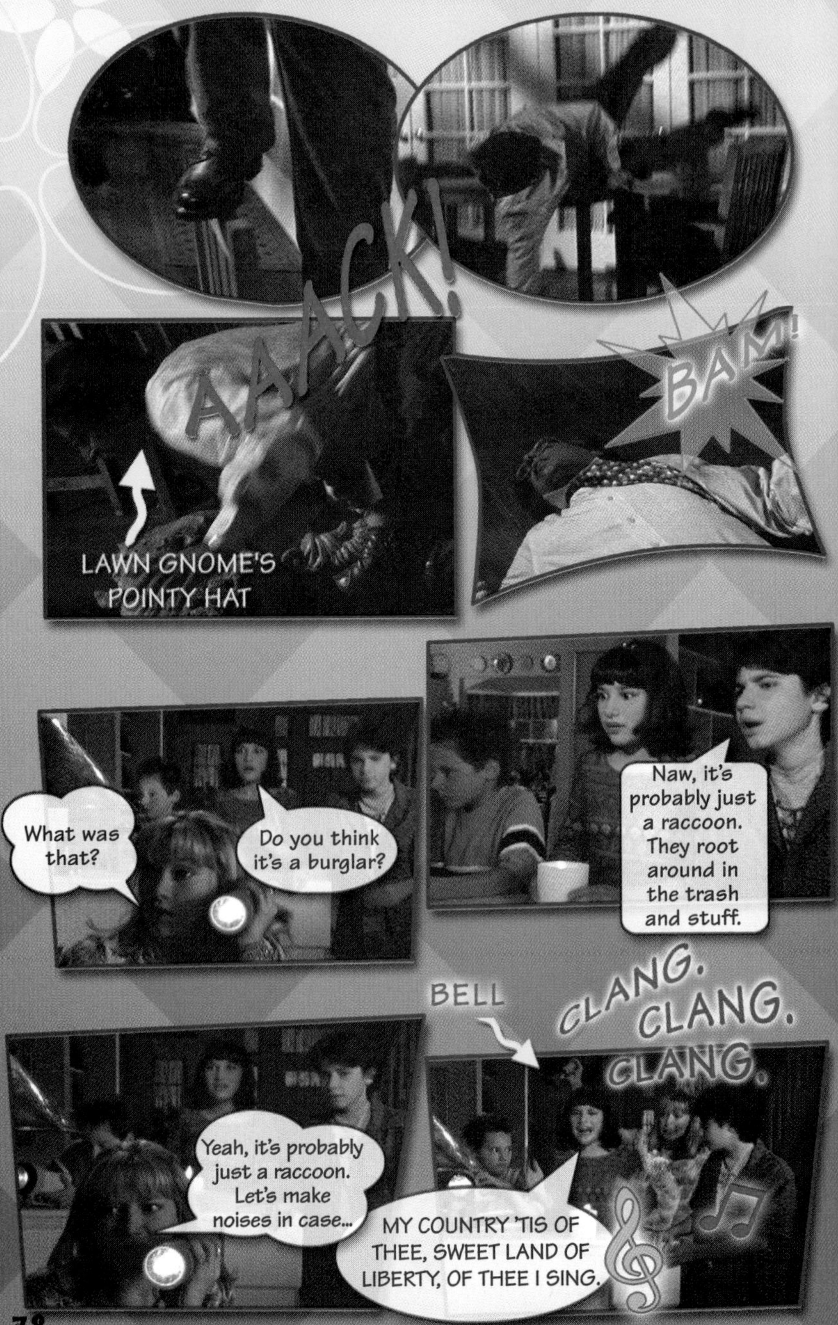
AAACK!
LAWN GNOME'S POINTY HAT
BAM!
What was that?
Do you think it's a burglar?
Naw, it's probably just a raccoon. They root around in the trash and stuff.
Yeah, it's probably just a raccoon. Let's make noises in case...
BELL
CLANG. CLANG. CLANG.
MY COUNTRY 'TIS OF THEE, SWEET LAND OF LIBERTY, OF THEE I SING.

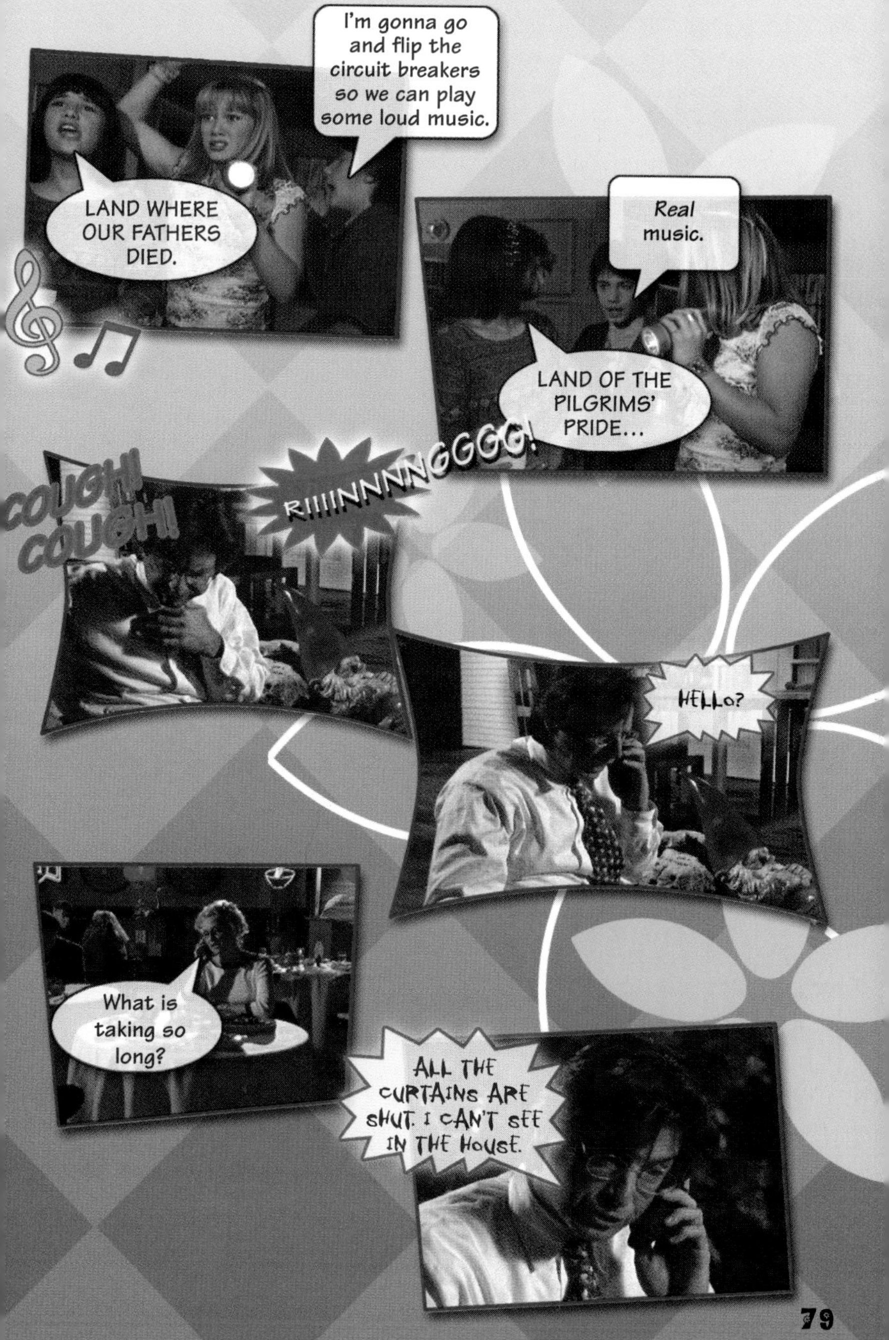

I'm gonna go and flip the circuit breakers so we can play some loud music.
LAND WHERE OUR FATHERS DIED.
Real music.
LAND OF THE PILGRIMS' PRIDE...
COUGH! COUGH!
RIIIINNNNNGGGG!
HELLO?
What is taking so long?
ALL THE CURTAINS ARE SHUT. I CAN'T SEE IN THE HOUSE.

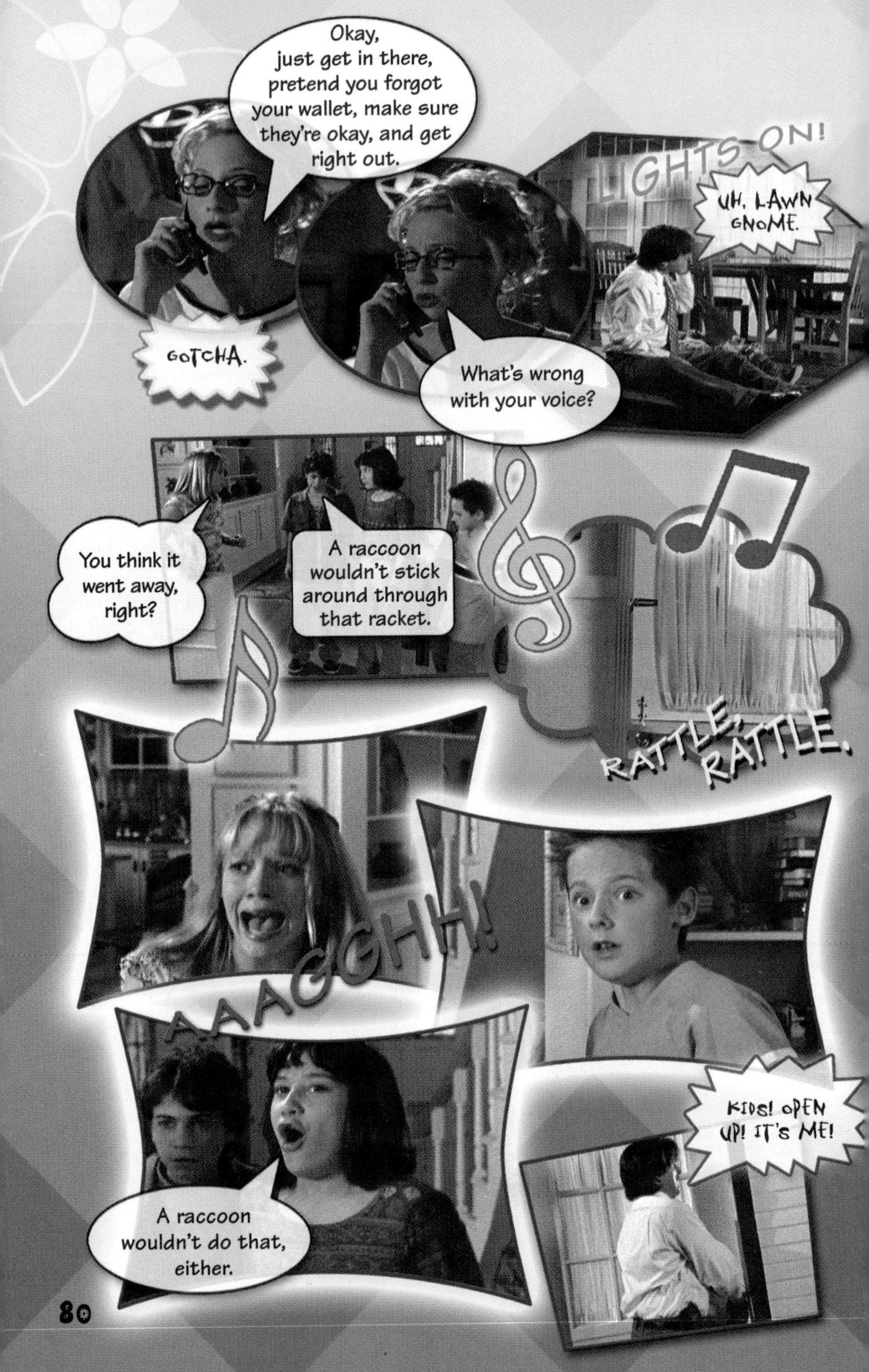
Okay, just get in there, pretend you forgot your wallet, make sure they're okay, and get right out.
GOTCHA.
What's wrong with your voice?
LIGHTS ON!
UH, LAWN GNOME.
You think it went away, right?
A raccoon wouldn't stick around through that racket.
RATTLE, RATTLE.
AAAGGHH!
A raccoon wouldn't do that, either.
KIDS! OPEN UP! IT'S ME!

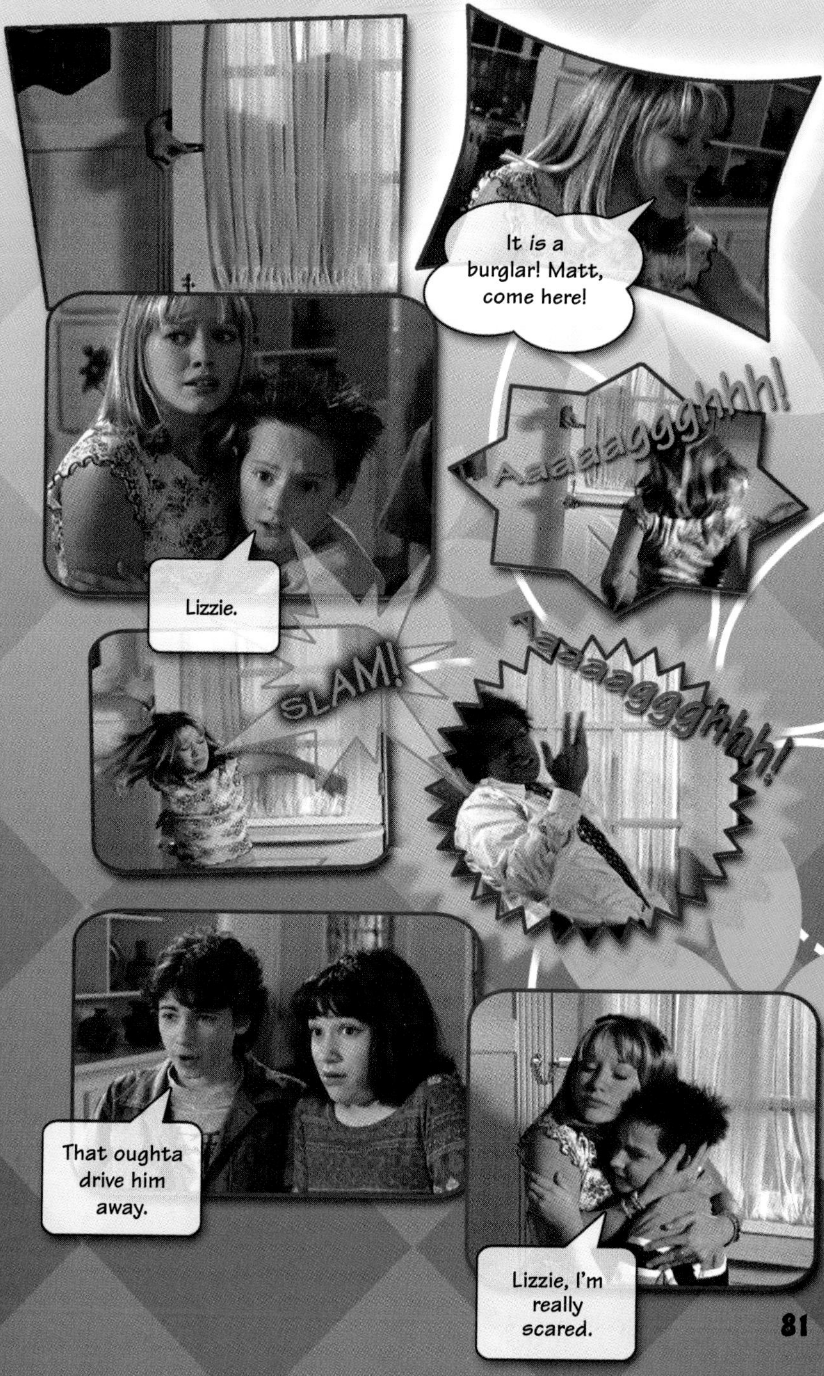
It is a burglar! Matt, come here!
Lizzie.
Aaaaaggghhh!
SLAM!
Aaaaaagggghhh!
That oughta drive him away.
Lizzie, I'm really scared.

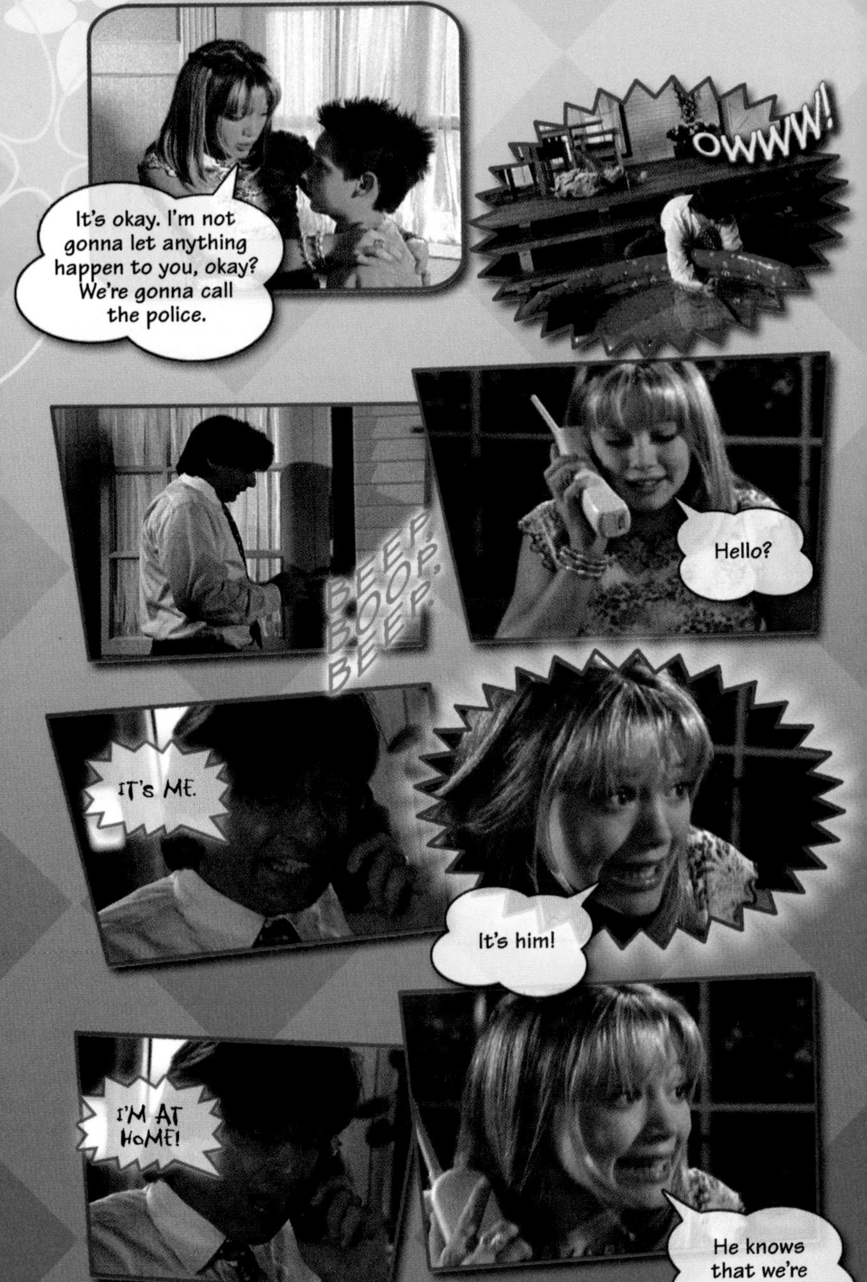
It's okay. I'm not gonna let anything happen to you, okay? We're gonna call the police.
OWWW!
BEEP, BOOP, BEEP
Hello?
IT'S ME.
It's him!
I'M AT HOME!
He knows that we're alone!

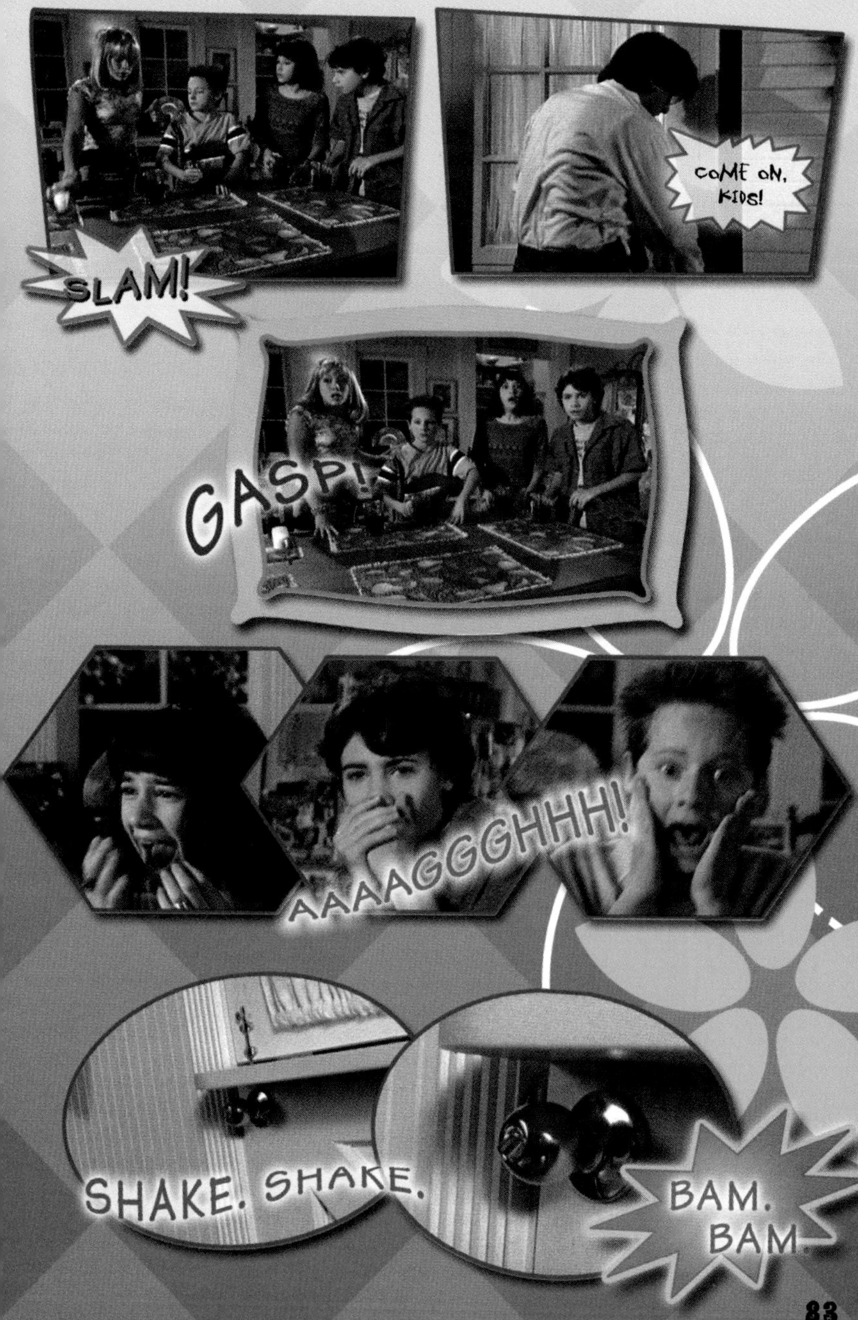
SLAM!
COME ON, KIDS!
GASP!
AAAAGGGHHH!
SHAKE. SHAKE.
BAM. BAM.

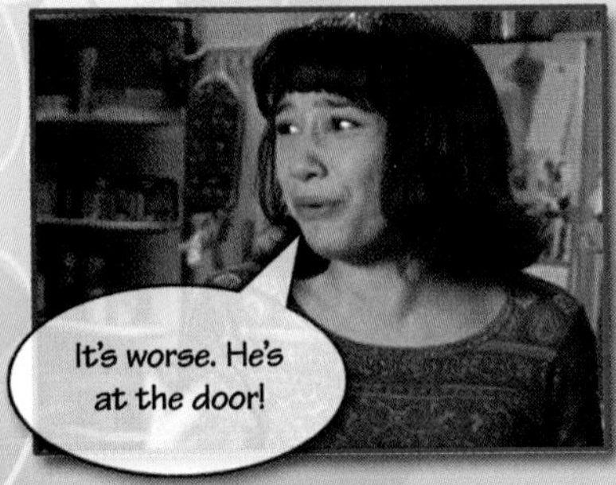
It's worse. He's at the door!

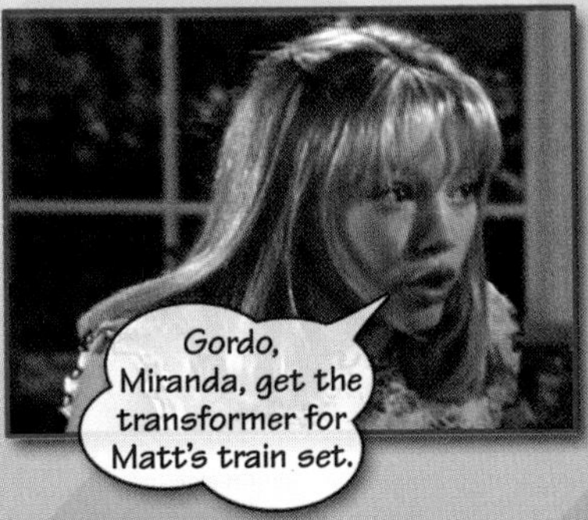
Gordo, Miranda, get the transformer for Matt's train set.

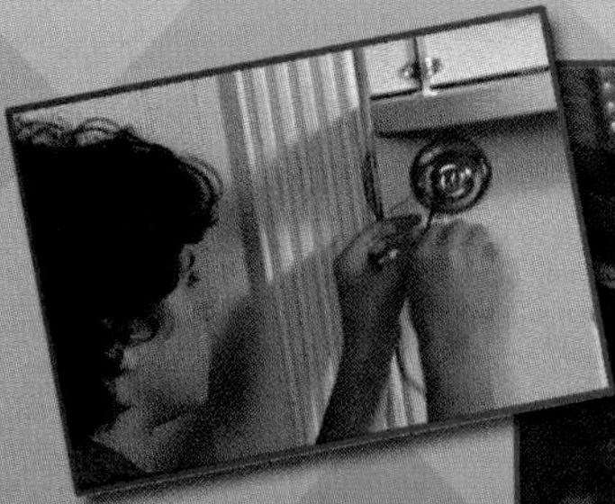

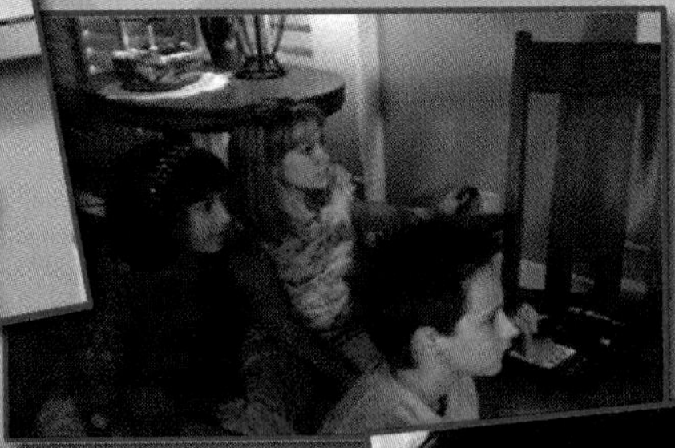

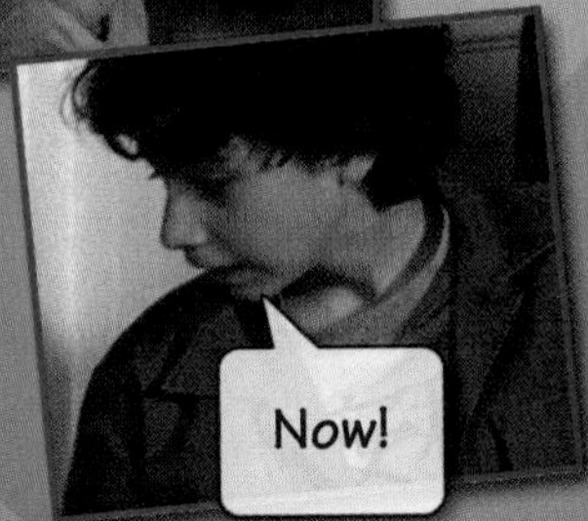
Now!

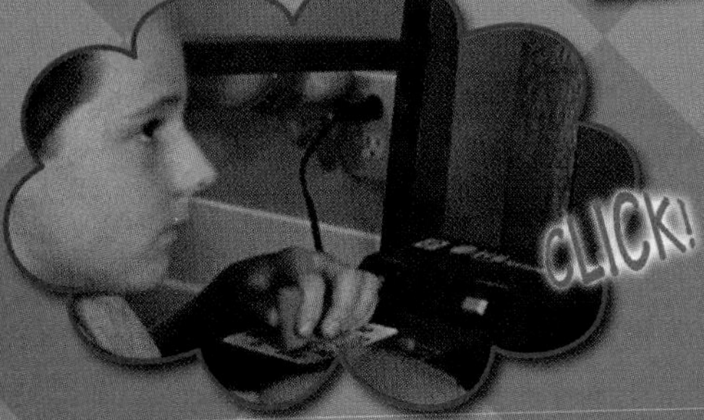
CLICK!

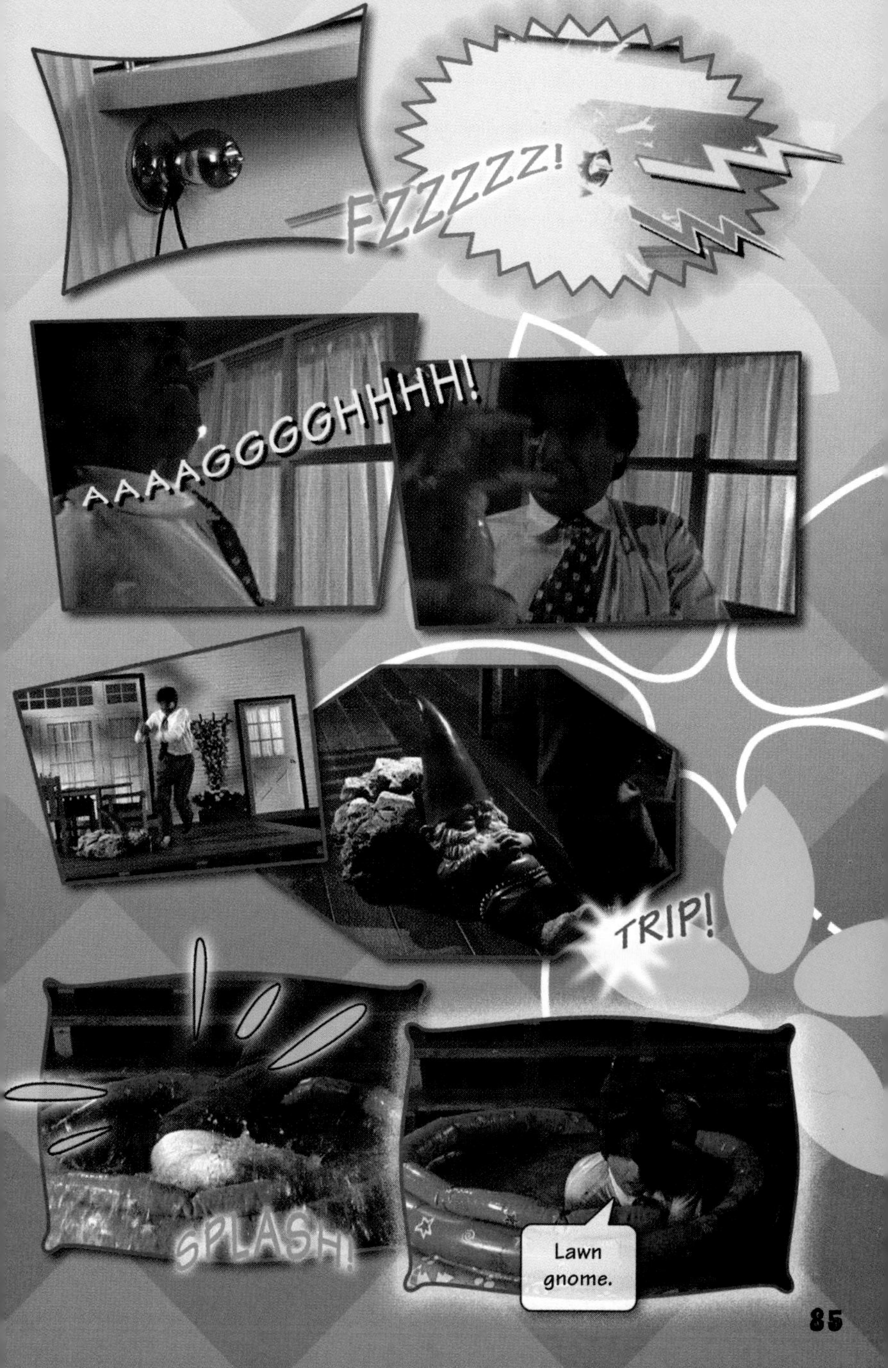

FZZZZZZ!
AAAAGGGGHHHHH!
TRIP!
SPLASH!
Lawn gnome.

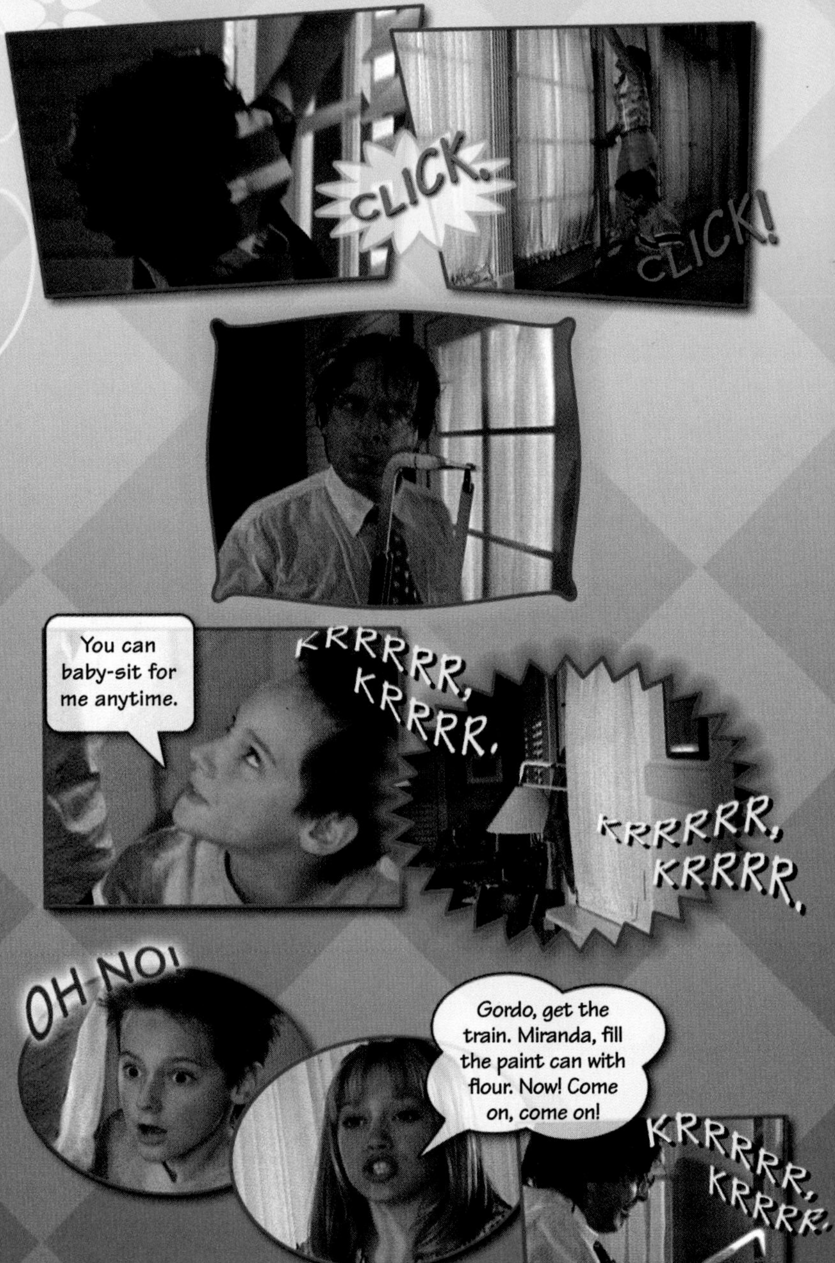
CLICK.
CLICK!
You can baby-sit for me anytime.
KRRRRRR, KRRRR.
KRRRRR, KRRRR.
OH NO!
Gordo, get the train. Miranda, fill the paint can with flour. Now! Come on, come on!
KRRRRRR, KRRRR.

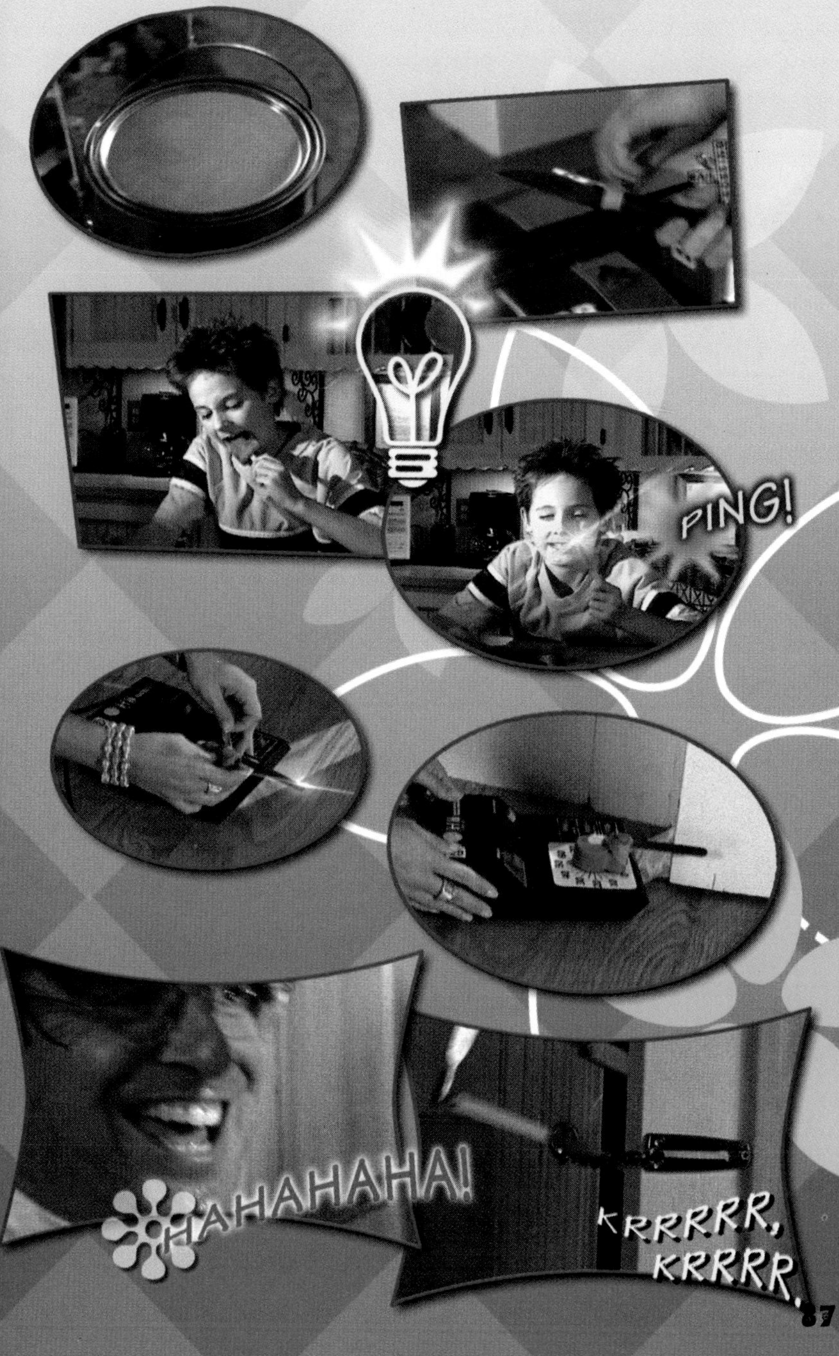
PING!
HAHAHAHA!
KRRRRR,
KRRRR...

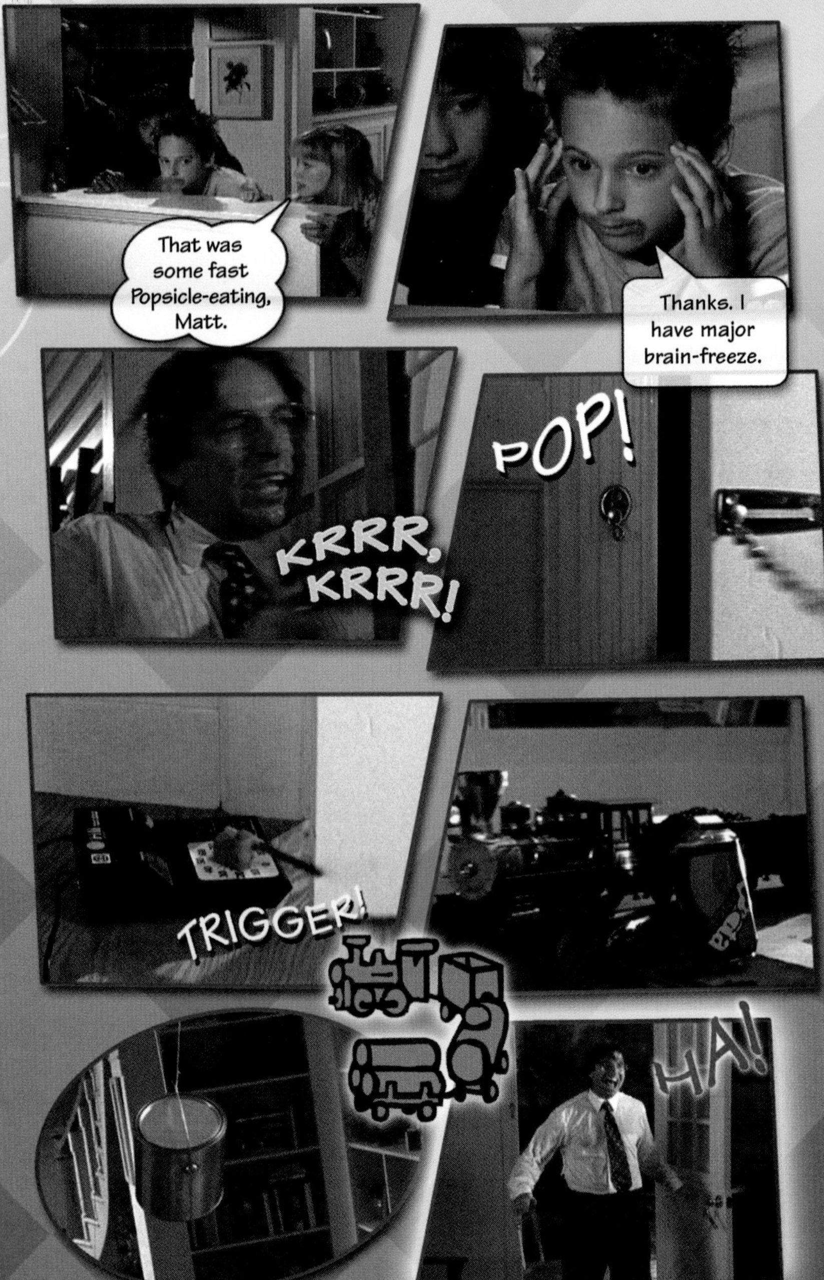
That was some fast Popsicle-eating, Matt.
Thanks. I have major brain-freeze.
KRRR, KRRR!
POP!
TRIGGER!
HA!

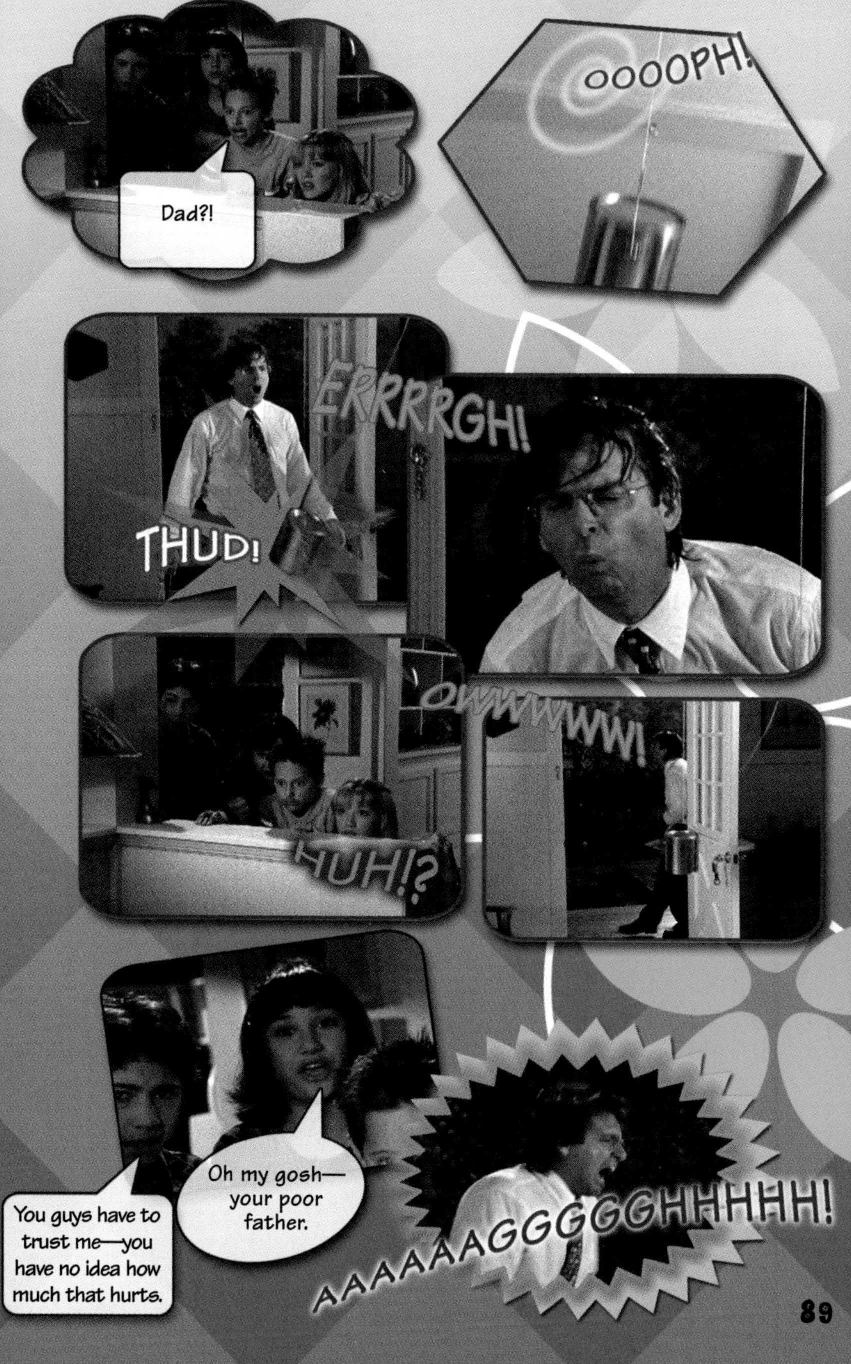

Dad?!
OOOOPH!
ERRRRGH!
THUD!
HUH!?
OWWWWWW!
You guys have to trust me—you have no idea how much that hurts.
Oh my gosh—your poor father.
AAAAAAGGGGGHHHHH!

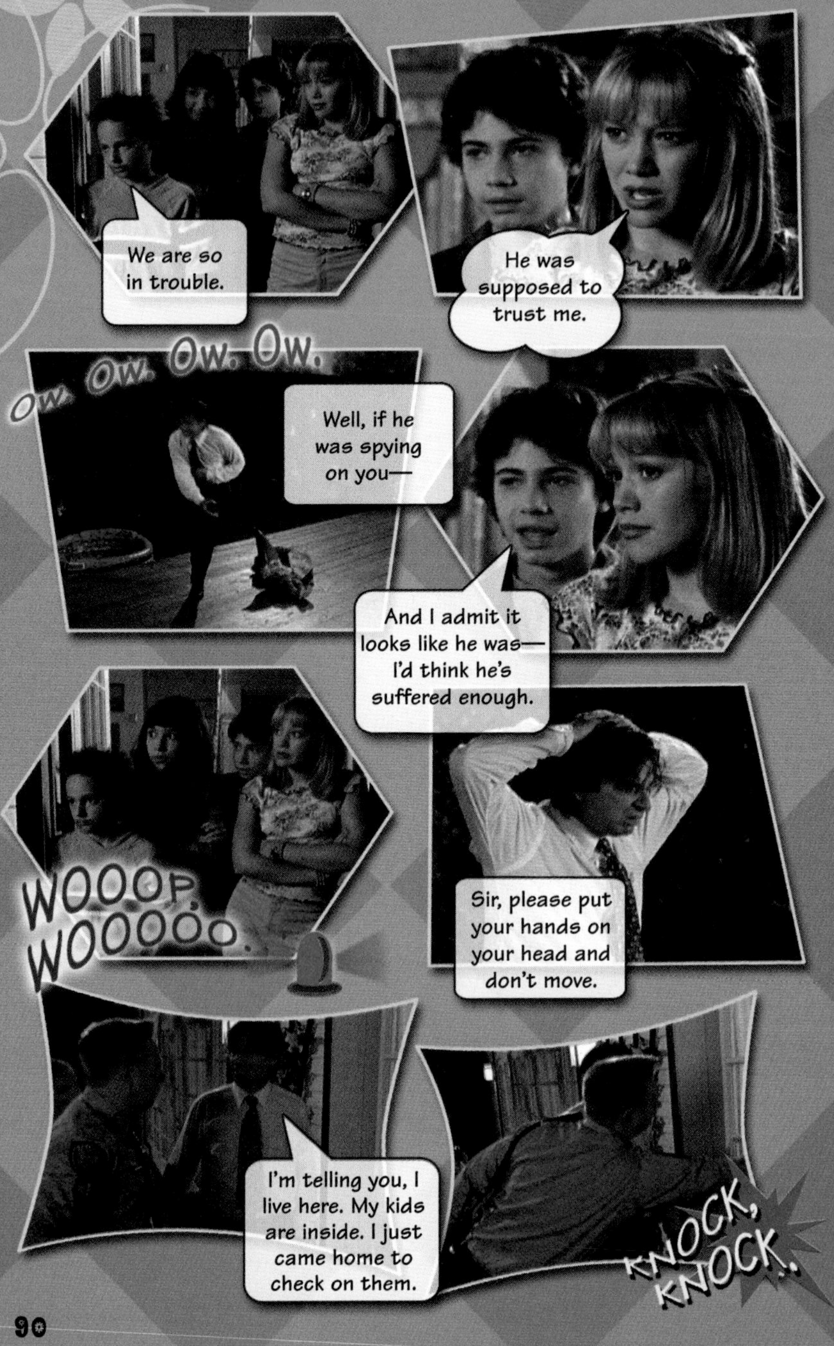
We are so in trouble.
He was supposed to trust me.
Ow. Ow. Ow. Ow.
Well, if he was spying on you—
And I admit it looks like he was— I'd think he's suffered enough.
WOOOP, WOOOOO.
Sir, please put your hands on your head and don't move.
I'm telling you, I live here. My kids are inside. I just came home to check on them.
KNOCK, KNOCK.

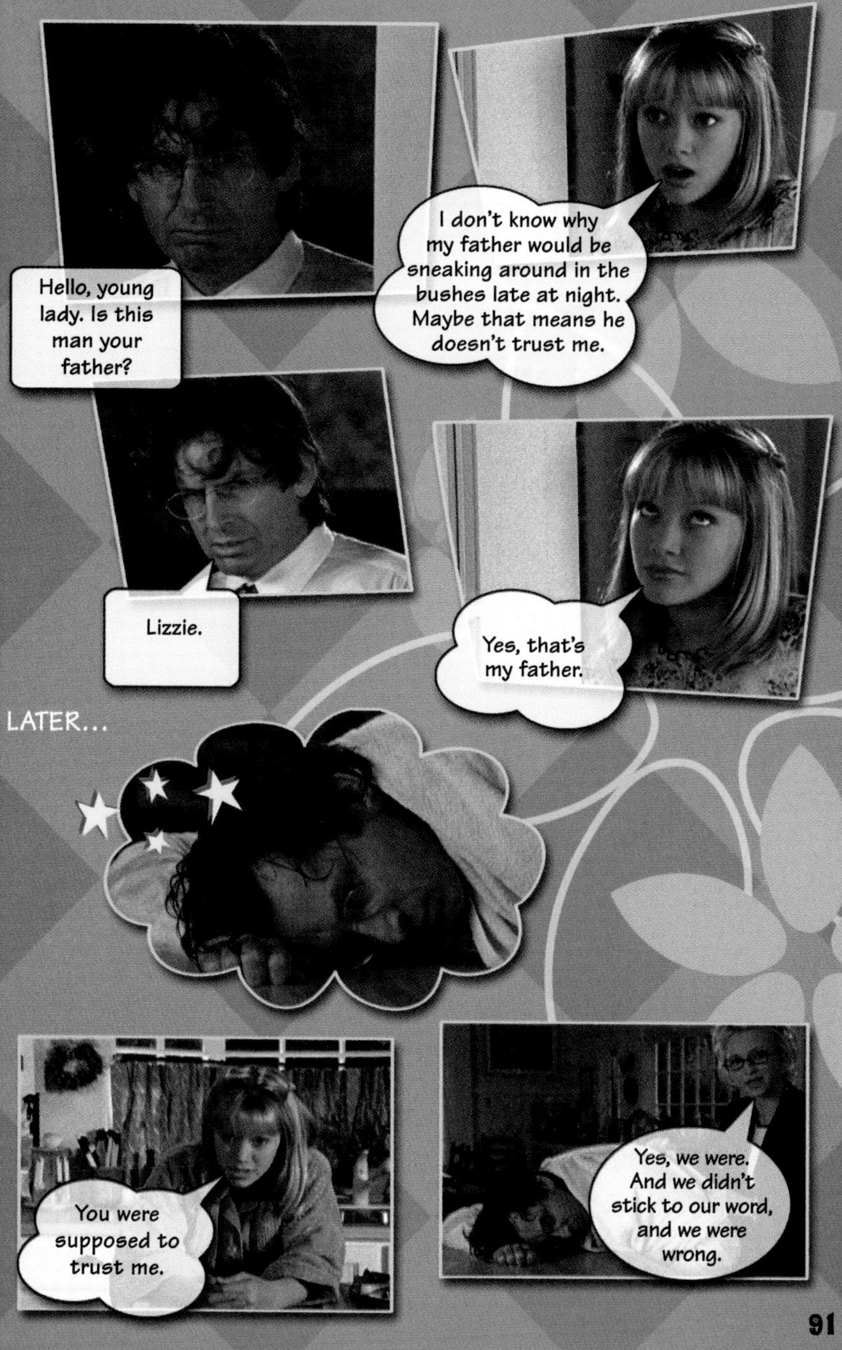
Hello, young lady. Is this man your father?
I don't know why my father would be sneaking around in the bushes late at night. Maybe that means he doesn't trust me.
Lizzie.
Yes, that's my father.
LATER...
You were supposed to trust me.
Yes, we were. And we didn't stick to our word, and we were wrong.

GASP!
They're admitting they were wrong?
Call the news crews. Film at eleven.
It's not that I don't trust you, sweetheart. I guess I still just think of you as the little six-year-old girl that used to need me to chase the monsters out of her closet. I guess I have to get used to the fact that you're not that little girl anymore. You're becoming a young lady and I have to let you act like one.
Can I go out on a real date?
No.
Will you teach me how to drive?
No.

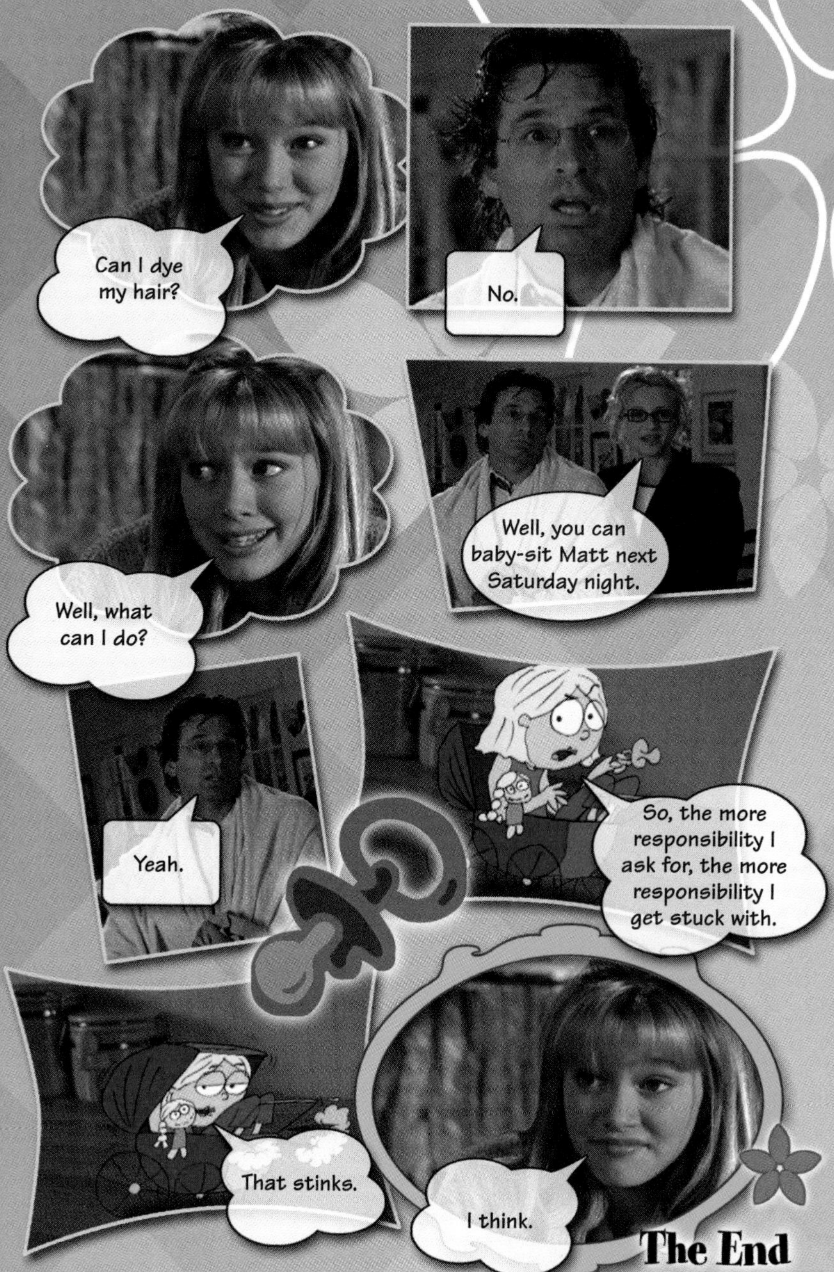
Can I dye my hair?
No.
Well, what can I do?
Well, you can baby-sit Matt next Saturday night.
Yeah.
So, the more responsibility I ask for, the more responsibility I get stuck with.
That stinks.
I think.
The End

Lizzie McGUiRE

CINE-MANGA™ VOLUME 4

COMING SOON FROM TOKYOPOP®

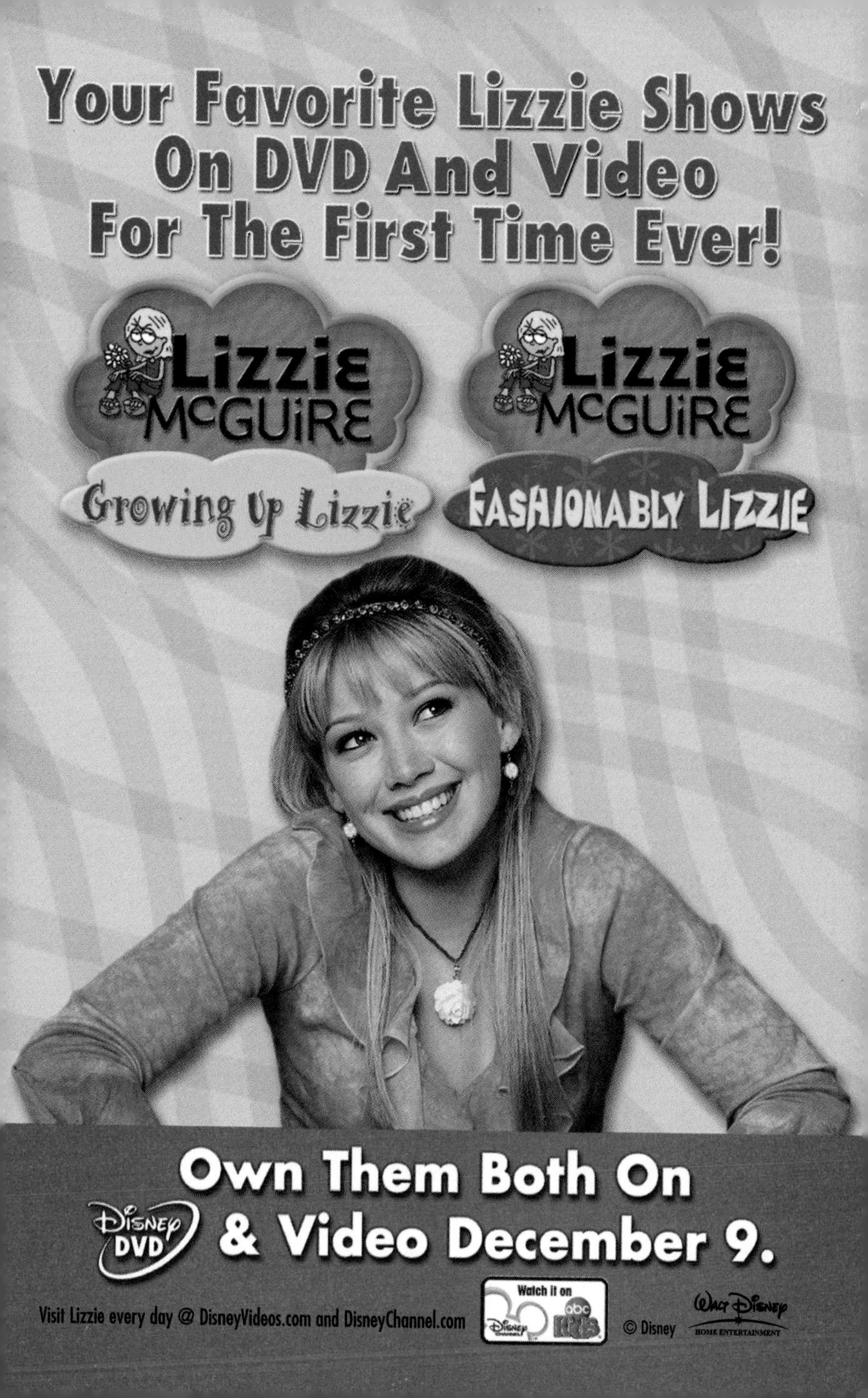
Your Favorite Lizzie Shows
On DVD And Video
For The First Time Ever!
Lizzie McGuire
Growing Up Lizzie
Lizzie McGuire
Fashionably Lizzie
Own Them Both On
Disney DVD
& Video December 9.
Visit Lizzie every day @ DisneyVideos.com and DisneyChannel.com
Watch it on
Disney Channel
abc Kids
© Disney
Walt Disney
Home Entertainment

Disney · PIXAR

FINDING NEMO

A
ALL AGES

CINE-MANGA™

AVAILABLE NOW FROM TOKYOPOP